FURTHER INTO THE GARDEN

DISCOVERING YOUR CHAKRAS

Companion to
Rebuilding the Garden

KARLA McLAREN

Laughing Tree
Press

Columbia, California

Book design by Columbine Type & Design.
Cover from the original painting by Ann Koziol.

This book presents powerful spiritual healing techniques for survivors of childhood sexual trauma. If you intend to use the information in this book, you must take this work seriously and with clear intent, or confusion may result. The author and publisher cannot assume liability or responsibility for actions inspired by information in this book. Since you are prescribing for yourself, use you own best discernment, or consult a holistic psychotherapist, medical expert, or trained healer for specific applications to your individual situation. Please, approach this work with due caution, spiritual intelligence, and a deep sense of personal responsibility.

First Printing 1997
Library of Congress Catalog Card Number: 97-93580
ISBN 0-9656583-1-7

This book is printed with soy-based inks on recycled paper.

CONTENTS

INTRODUCTION

Hello again, and welcome to all you Gardeners who want to dig further into your intuitive abilities. I'd like to get right into the fascinating topic of the *chakras*, but first, a caveat: this book is not meant to stand alone. It relies heavily on the grounding, separating, emotional channelling, and healing skills you learned in *Rebuilding the Garden*, and moves on swiftly from there. I don't want to waste our time or any paper here re-explaining something we should already know.

This book is a gift to my Garden readers—it is meant only for survivors of childhood sexual assault who have their basic healing skills under them. If you picked up this book by mistake and are interested in starting from the beginning with your *chakras*, please refer to my book for non-Garden readers: *Your Aura and Your Chakras: The Owner's Manual*. Thank you.

DISCOVERING YOUR CHAKRAS

Beyond sculptures and symphonies,
beyond great works and masterpieces,
is the greater, finer art of molding a conscious life.
Genius appears everywhere,
but never so magnificently
as in a life well lived.

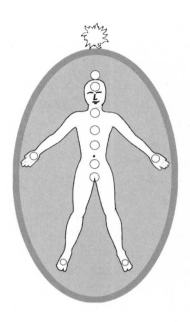

FURTHER INTO THE GARDEN

WELCOME BACK

I'm excited to welcome you to this book on the *chakras*, because understanding your *chakras* can help you become a powerful self-healer. All the skills you learned in *Rebuilding the Garden* helped you to understand your actions and reactions in the world around you; now, working with your *chakras* will help you to understand your inner self.

If you are wondering why I kept the *chakras* out of *Rebuilding the Garden*, it was not because they were less important than any other topic. I kept them out because I didn't want to bring up the *chakras* until you had gotten fairly comfortable with your intuitive reading

2 FURTHER INTO THE GARDEN

and healing skills. It is important to have a functional aura before you begin to work with your chakras.

If you can see the aura as your energetic skin, and the *chakras* as your energetic glands and organs, you'll begin to understand the primary need for a healthy aura. If your skin isn't whole, your organs and glands will be at constant, life-threatening risk. When your skin is strong, your glands and organs will be protected. If your aura-care and grounding skills are weak, your *chakras* will be at constant risk. Any *chakra* work done before the aura is whole is essentially a waste of your time.

Being able to read and heal and understand what your *chakras* are doing will be immensely useful to you now, but it would have been too confusing during your beginning studies. Besides, the *chakra* information made the main *Garden* book too long. Instead of lightly skimming over the *chakras* in deference to space, I decided to separate the *chakras* from the main book to give them the coverage they deserve.

Chakra is the Sanskrit word for a series of circular energy centers in and around the body. However, we will now accept the word into the English language so I won't have to go crazy italicizing the word throughout this entire book. If there were an English word that was even close in meaning, I would have used it.

There are chakras, or energy centers, in the palms of your hands and on the soles of your feet, and there are seven central chakras lined up the center of your body. The eighth chakra, your Gold Sun, hovers right above you, just outside the upper edge of your aura. Our body grounding cords originate in the lower-most central chakra, the first chakra. See my illustration for the location of each of the chakras.

Many Eastern religions offer a great deal of information about the chakras. Their seven central chakras have seven different names, each with its own musical note, color, shape, animal, gland, and so forth. All these classifications are interesting, but just as it is with the aura and the body, one could spend years studying all the possible functions, meanings, and historical theories of the chakras without ever learning to work with them in simple, useful ways. I will not spend much time on such list-like classifications, because they take attention away from basic healing.

In the most rudimentary definition, chakras are a kind of place-holder for specific spirit/body abilities. It is almost as if the chakras are gauges or meters that can tell us about the relative health of the ability in question.

For instance, if I want to know about a person's ability to work with spiritual information, I will look at the chakra just above her head (the seventh chakra) to see how open and healthy it is. If I want to look at her ability to balance spirit, body, and self-healing, I'll focus on her heart chakra (the fourth chakra). If I want to see how well her immune system is working, both physically and spiritually, I'll look at her solar plexus (the third chakra).

There are certainly other ways to get this information, such as studying aura skews and so forth (or through psychotherapy to some extent, or by asking the person directly), but when I want to get to the root of any spiritual difficulty, I'll focus my attention on the chakras.

Energy troubles in the aura are a reflection of what is going on with us, but the root cause of the troubles can usually be found inside one of our chakras. We can puff out a portion of our auras, or heal an aura skew a number of times, but if we don't look at what is going on in our chakras, we may just be applying Band-Aids to a significant and ongoing energy problem.

If we, for instance, must constantly place gift symbols or Sentries in front of our first chakra area—or we can't stay grounded—we must examine our first chakra to get to the root of the difficulty. Otherwise, we'll probably overlook the main issue, and merely perform damage control with our external energy tools.

Or, if our aura boundary is constantly hazy and our Sentry doesn't function, those are clear signs that our protective third chakra is not functioning, and needs a healing. We would need to look at our third chakra in order to address our auric immune system breakdown.

Working with each of our chakras, now that we have some experience of grounding, separating, reading, and healing, will help us to further separate from our molest experience. Through reading our auras, we were able to get an overview of our energy strengths and weaknesses; we learned how we function. Now, when we read our chakras, we can zero in on the foundational energies that determine *why* we function in the ways that we do.

To get us easily and instantly into the chakra system, I'll start with a quick chakra-check reading. Then, I'll devote a chapter to each of the chakras, describe an involved reading, and show you a simple way to cleanse and align your chakras during your regular Gold Sun healing. At the very end of this book, I will also cover the topic of *cording*, which is the energetic form a relationship contract often takes.

AND NOW, THE WARNING: Students in any discipline often develop a group narcissism that helps them to feel special, and separate from the unwashed, untutored masses. Don't be surprised if you get a little cocky about healing your chakras when everyone else around you is unaware (in your opinion) and spiritually undeveloped. But, don't get married to your superiority. You'll be stupid again, don't worry.

If you study your chakras in a healthy way, you will bring forth more questions. Sometimes, the things you see in your chakras will make you want to collapse and leave your training behind. You won't feel superior; you'll feel like a dope. This is good. It's a sign that you are growing past old ways of acting and reacting (where you were superior to the information), and making way for new information (which is naturally superior to you until you integrate it).

When your learning takes you off in too many directions, go back to the beginning. Keep grounding. Re-read the earliest parts of *Rebuilding the Garden*. Go over the Troubleshooting Guide again, and keep things simple.

When you are once again grounded and not so cocky, go back to the place where you were overwhelmed. You will find that you can come at the issue differently. By keeping your feet on the ground, you will be able to learn to fly. When you can fly through your issues, you won't have time to look down on other people.

Remember, everyone has an aura and chakras. Many people can maintain their spiritual health without ever learning anything about them. We had to go back to the beginning and learn about our spiritual bodies because of our molest experience. We shouldn't assume that other people's chakras are not healthy just because they have never heard of chakras. Other people have other paths, that's all.

Oh, and another thing: if you've read other books about the chakras, this information may contradict what you have already learned. My only comment is this: I've never read a book on the chakras. Whatever I know about chakras was learned on the job, from the chakras themselves. I heard some information on the chakra's colors and locations in a class once, and started healing them soon after.

This book is not a treatise about the chakras; it is a narrative translated directly from the world of the chakras. Hopefully, it will lead you into the world of your own chakras, where you will be able to discern any discrepancies for yourself.

Be Aware: If you are using drugs, alcohol, caffeine, or tobacco, either recreationally or medicinally, your chakra function will be disrupted. Depending on the drugs you choose, your chakras may be slightly impaired, selectively damaged, or essentially non-functional.

Recovering from drug use can be a lengthy process, but attending to the damage in your chakras will help to pull you out of the drug twilight-zone. If you are ready to move away from drugs, please see an energy-centered physician such as an acupuncturist. Detoxify, attend to your nutritional needs, look into the Bach Flower Remedies, and give your poor body a chance to rebuild. When you are cleaner, you will benefit from the information in this book.

Please know that none of the work, in this book or *Rebuilding the Garden*, will be effective against an onslaught of drugs. If you cannot free yourself from drug use, *put this book down*. It is not safe for you to work with your chakras yet, because you won't be able to stay grounded or in the room in your head. You won't be able to maintain a strong aura, and your chakras will be at risk.

At this moment in time, drug use and other addiction-distractions are absolutely epidemic. As a result, most of us have very poor attention spans, and very little ability to withstand the natural discomforts inherent in growth and learning. Some spiritual teachers, in capitulation, I guess, are promoting drug use as an entry into other realms.

I can understand the frustration that would lead a spiritual teacher to capitulate to drug use in their students. I can't, however, recommend or support the practice. Though I tried to keep an open mind about drug use in my early healing career, I never worked on a drug-user whose aura or chakras were at all healthy. Drug use creates blown-out chakras, jagged, shattered auras, and very poor body-spirit communication. Even alcohol, caffeine and cigarettes distort and disrupt the energy body.

I now limit my practice so that I don't work on or with drug users. I have found the energy scattering and disruption that go hand-in-hand with drug use makes grounding and centering nearly impossible. Without those two abilities, this work can't proceed.

The higher, or alternate, realms do exist, and they can be accessed through drug use. But, they can also be accessed—drug-free—through grounding and centering, and through sincere application and integrity. The latter way is clearly my way.

It is very important to understand the difference between the transcendental path, and a transformational one. Transcendentalists wish to leave behind the shackles of the body, the emotions, and even the mind. The transcendental path skews almost completely to the spiritual quadrant of the quaternity of mind, body, spirit, and emotion. Drug use and certain meditative practices can help transcendentalists achieve that skew.

Transformationalists wish to live spiritual lives with their bodies, their minds, and their emotional selves intact. The transformational path does not skew toward any quadrant; its intention is to create cohesion and cooperation between all four parts of the quaternity. Both paths have their place, but this book, and this teaching, are about the transformational path.

Though I know some teachers may tell you otherwise, the truth is that recreational drug use has no place in competent, grounded, transformational spiritual healing.

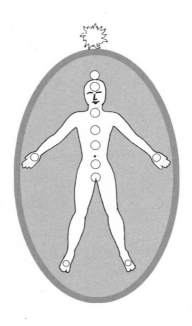

FURTHER INTO THE GARDEN

THE CHAKRA CHECK

Before you start to read or study your chakras, it's always a good idea to give them a mini-healing first. The chakras, like the aura, have a certain basic form, and if this form can be established before a reading, the reading will flow more smoothly.

I envision each chakra as a forward-facing disk of swirling energy. Healthy central chakras are usually anywhere from three to five inches in diameter, while the hand and feet chakras are generally somewhat smaller (two to three inches) in diameter. In depth, chakras can range from a cylindrical length of two to three inches to as much as a foot, depending on the energy output of their owner. Longer chakras equal more energy, while shorter chakras equal less.

In healthy chakras, I look for a clearly delineated, circular border; a clean and healthy color that is specific to the chakra; and a constant, gentle flow of energy within the chakra. Deviations from this norm are to be expected and even celebrated in early chakra healings and readings. They mean both that you are becoming a good reader, and that your chakras are aware enough to send you messages about their difficulties.

Chakras, like auras, are extremely active and busy. If you don't clear them out and get them calmed down before you start to read, you could easily spend an hour on each chakra as it tells you stories of past, present, and future. The stories are fascinating, but not always valid to you in the present moment, and not always directive as to what you can do to alleviate any difficulties you might find.

The healing I call the Chakra Check is a simple way to remind the chakras about their ideal shape, size, and color. During a subsequent reading or healing, your Chakra-Checked chakras can show you any deviations they are experiencing right now, as opposed to deviations they have experienced in the past or will experience in the future. The Chakra Check cleans your chakras out and pulls them into present time; it calls them to attention.

During the Chakra Check, it is important to remember that you are at this point *telling* your chakras what to do, and not listening to their stories. If you stop and listen to them at this point, your Chakra Check will not be a quick healing, but a time-consuming reading. You must be in a directive attitude here instead of a receptive one. Receptivity will be called for in the actual chakra studies and readings to follow.

Starting with your eighth chakra, right above your aura, envision this energy center as an open and shining Gold Sun, filled with a metallic golden light. Stay inside your head.

At your seventh chakra, right above the crown of your head, envision a healthy, open, circular and defined energy center filled with a clear, flowing, lively, jewel-like purple-violet energy. See this chakra, and all your central chakras, opened to a three-to-five-inch diameter.

Now direct your attention to your forehead and see your sixth chakra (or third eye) as healthy, open, circular, and defined. See it filled with a clear, moving, vibrant, sparkling indigo energy.

As you shift your attention down to your fifth, or throat, chakra (just above that depression at the base of your throat) see this chakra filled with a clear, moving, bright sapphire-blue energy. Stay in the room in your head. Do not fly out of your head to visit each of your chakras. You can see them just fine from inside your head.

Center your attention on your fourth or heart chakra (which is centered over your sternum). Remind it to be healthy, open to the same diameter as your upper three chakras, circular and defined, and filled with a clear, moving, light emerald-green energy.

Your third chakra, at your solar plexus, should be healthy and open, circular and defined, and filled with a clear, flowing, bright and sunny yellow energy.

Now see your second chakra (just below your navel) as healthy and open, circular and defined, and filled with a clear, moving, shimmering persimmonny-orange color.

Stay in your head and envision your first chakra (just above the testicles in men, or at the low-center of the vagina in women) as an open, healthy, and defined energy center filled with a clear, moving, sparkling, light ruby-red energy. Make sure to include a picture of your healthy grounding cord in your vision of your first chakra.

See your hand chakras (in the center of your palms) open to two or three inches in diameter, and see your feet chakras (in the center of your arches, facing downward toward the earth) open to those dimensions as well. Do not assign colors to your hands and feet, but be aware of any colors already present.

That's it. Now your chakras are awake and aware of what they're *supposed* to be doing. Though you can go on to study or heal them now, this Chakra Check is an excellent mini-healing. You can perform this healing at any time, whether you are intending to go on to a full chakra reading or not.

If you do go on to read your chakras after this quick tune-up, your reading will be much more valid and reality-based, because your extremely active and busy chakras will be calmed and centered. If you don't go on to a full reading, your chakras will be happy anyway, because this mini-healing gets them back into alignment and connection, with you and with each other. Like you, your chakras love to be noticed and talked to, even in seemingly inconsequential ways.

Read through the following descriptions of each chakra and try a reading or a healing. Remember that any deviation or damage you see in your chakras is a sign that you are becoming a competent, aware chakra owner who sees the truth. The deviations you see are not a sign of failure or spiritual stupidity; they are signs that you are a good intuitive reader, and that it's time to get to work. Remind yourself that you are now an intuitive healer. You can deal with any problems your chakras share with you.

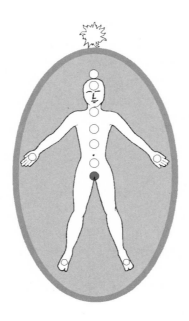

FURTHER INTO THE GARDEN

THE FIRST (OR KUNDALINI) CHAKRA

This bright red, expressive chakra (all odd-numbered chakras are primarily expressive, all evens are primarily receptive) is located at the very base of the spine, just inside the vagina in women, and just above the testicles in men. The first chakra is the chakra of basic survival, the primal sex drive, and bodily life energy.

The first chakra is (or should be) connected to the chakras in the soles of the feet. If this connection is not healthy, grounding may be very difficult. In any study of the first chakra, the feet chakras must be included as well. Please refer to the chapter on the feet chakras later in this book for an in-depth look at the connection between the two.

The energy of basic survival is very powerful. When first chakra, or *kundalini* energy runs upward and through the body (the first is the only chakra that does this naturally), its intensity can help to ensure physical survival in the face of danger. First chakra energy is responsible for sudden bursts of strength; it can help people run from or competently face violent encounters, or lift trucks off of small children.

Kundalini energy will also flow upward in some instances of spiritual awakening. Because of this, many spiritual groups have worked out techniques to get the *kundalini* to run upward even when there has been no awakening, and there is no danger. When the *kundalini* runs upward, it blasts up and through each of the other six central chakras and out of the head, like a cobra ready to strike.

The physical sensations resulting from this upward flow are very much like a cocaine rush. One feels invincible, extremely wakeful and alert, psychically aware, and totally uninterested in food, sleep, or any other mundane life process. It is a good feeling for a while, but running the *kundalini* to get it has its consequences.

I can't begin to count the number of jumpy, ungrounded, exhausted people who have come to me to have their *kundalini* re-routed. A little bit of first chakra energy goes a very long way, and after a while, the body can't handle all of the energy, not to mention the food and sleep deprivation.

Kundalini meditations used by advanced and centered yogis can bring about healing evolution; however, many *kundalini* teachings in the West are not taught by or to advanced yogis. Here, *kundalini* work is often like recreational drug abuse; using the *kundalini* energy starts out as a really exciting idea, then turns into a catastrophe.

If people are not completely sure of how they managed to raise their *kundalini* (usually, one chants and fasts and sits in deep meditation until the first chakra wakes up and starts blasting), they won't be able to lower it with any certainty, either. Coming out of meditation and eating again does not always work.

Interestingly, cults use chanting, food deprivation, and sleep deprivation to bring recruits into the fold, all of which will send the *kundalini* up and out (the *kundalini* normally activates itself, as a protection, in times of starvation and insomnia). For Westerners who have no experience of spiritual or psychic energy, this *kundalini* rush can be overwhelming. Instead of acknowledging their own first chakra's power, they give their power to the cult and the cult experience, which is what helps create the entrapping culture.

If people are not allowed to explore or experience the energy of their own spirituality, they are perfect prey for cults, gurus, and anything else that offers the illusion of power and spiritual knowledge.

Even though the *kundalini* energy can cause many problems, the first chakra is actually very responsive. It's very easy to re-route, even if it's been running up and out of the head for a very long time.

One of the worst cases I ever saw was a female cult member who had kept her first chakra blasting upward for so long that she had broken out in an all-over red rash. It looked just like her skin had been burnt. The fire of the *kundalini* was actually beginning to burn her skin.

This woman came to me for a healing, so I grounded her and created a blue moon (see the *Kundalini* Healing in *Rebuilding the Garden's* Troubleshooting Guide) above her head. Almost immediately, she went into a series of seizures as she re-entered her body and her first chakra energy drained out of each of her upper chakras. I kept working, and the seizures stopped when her first chakra energy got back into its own place again. Now, she was crying in big, racking sobs, but we kept working, and soon she was grounding from her first chakra again, and her energy had evened out. Her upper chakras were damaged and distorted because they had been forced to run first chakra vibrations instead of their own, but we soon got them back to normal.

She told me it was like waking up from a dream that had turned into an endless, hallucinatory nightmare. She felt that she had been seduced and then trapped in another world. Her cult was one that fell apart in a big, ugly way a few years later, leaving many wounded people in its wake. She was relieved to have gotten out when she did, even though she was vilified for doing so by people she thought were her "family."

The rash went away the day after our first healing, and she was able to resume her life as a wiser and more centered, if somewhat less idealistic, person.

If left to its own devices, the first chakra will turn its *kundalini* rushes on and off. Triggering events can be danger or emergency, illness and depression, or an opening into spiritual awareness. In these instances, the energy of the first chakra will channel itself up and through the other chakras as a kind of wake-up call.

When the first chakra turns itself on in response to real-need situations such as these, it will turn itself off in its own time, without any help. The *kundalini* energy is very self-governing, and it knows more than we do about its own functioning and responsibilities.

I would not suggest playing with the *kundalini* as if it were a toy or a drug, or using it to take a shortcut to spiritual awareness. It might be fun to play with the power of the *kundalini* for a while, but it wreaks havoc in the other chakras, which cannot function very long at the vibrational level of the first chakra. The blasting can also damage the aura, which will not remain healthy if it is only allowed to have one color (red) and one frequency of vibrational energy. Added to those two serious drawbacks is the fact that it is almost impossible to ground when the first chakra energy is running upward.

We molest survivors, in most cases, do not have a good relationship with our first chakras. Most of us run a lot of cobra-like striking anger, which is a *kundalini* rush signalling distress. Either that, or we feel listless and suicidal, which is a sign of a low survival instinct and a shut-off first chakra (no *kundalini* energy at all). The reason for this imbalance is that our first chakra energy was used against us as children, and turned up to an adult level of openness far too soon.

Little bodies have, in most cases, little chakras. Until kids are thirteen, their chakras run at a lower energy level. Their parents' energy still guides and feeds them to some extent. Molest opens the crucial survival chakra too wide for the child to adequately control it, while the molester feeds off the damaged chakra's sexual and life energy like a parasite. Both molesters and molest survivors often over-run or close off their own first chakras in response to their sense of being cut off from their own basic survival energy.

People who choose to molest others deal with their loss of first chakra energy by cording into (see the chapter called *Special Topic: Cording*) and stealing the first chakra energy of unprotected people. The unprotected may be children, powerless people in the molester's family, older people with poor psychic boundaries, or people with limited mental and emotional capabilities. Often, a molester will unconsciously attach a psychic leash or cord between her first chakra and the first chakra of her victim. This cord connects the molester and the victim years and sometimes decades beyond the actual event.

This energy remnant of the molesting sexual encounter confers a kind of abusive programming in the vital first chakra that makes healing (and healing sexuality) nearly impossible. Remember that the first chakra will do whatever we tell it to do. If someone we bond with (and there is a bond with sexual partners, even if the sex is forced on us) has told our first chakra to stay uncomfortably open and available for abuse, it will do that.

We may subconsciously see or feel the ugliness in our first chakra. We may try to shut it down in response, but it will yo-yo back open as soon as we're not looking. The first chakra will continue in this pattern until we change its destructive programming, which is very easy to do with energy work.

We ground from our first chakra in order to drain out any old cords and messages that may be left over from our molestation. When we are able to work with and clean out our first chakra energy, many of the symptoms of reactive survival lessen in intensity, because much of the old molestation programming becomes dislodged.

Suicidal urges become more manageable as we learn to live in our bodies without the self-hatred that stems from a total lack of peace, safety, and grounding. The rage we channel becomes more directed as our surging *kundalini* energy lowers itself and comes within our conscious control. In response, our auras become calmer, and the flashing memories slow down to allow us to catch up and process them. We also become more able to stay in our body during sex. We may even begin to enjoy ourselves.

When we get in touch with the energy of our basic survival and sexuality, we remove the ugly assault energy from our first chakra. Grounding then becomes a welcome, restful, relieving treat. Our first chakras become a healing foundation for us instead of something that only serves to remind us of our assault.

When we can comfortably sit in our own pelvis again, our groundedness will allow us to stay in our head, clean out our aura, define our boundaries, and separate from others responsibly. Clearing out our first chakra also gets us back in touch with its version of frank, natural, and completely necessary sexuality, which is fun when balanced with the other chakras' versions of sex, but rather excessive all by itself.

Many molest memories and contracts are stored in the first chakra. As your awareness increases, more molest-contract and molest-programming information will be released into your conscious mind. This is spectacularly good, because it means that you are moving to ever deeper levels of awareness and healing. Keep grounding and clearing out, burn your contracts and channel your emotions, and watch as your spirit starts to take flight. It all starts with your healthy first chakra.

OPEN OR CLOSED FIRST CHAKRA

Along with any first chakra problem, a linked difficulty may appear in (or originate from) the feet chakras. Since the feet chakras should be connected to the first, please include the feet chakras in your study or healing of the first chakra. Healthy feet chakras will support any first chakra work you do. The feet chakras are covered later in this book.

A very large and open first chakra is usually a sign that a person is in basic survival mode. The survival energy can come from financial, emotional, or physical distress.

If you are right in the middle of a catastrophe, let your first chakra remain large so that it can assist you, but be aware that it may start running upward in a *kundalini* rush. Your first chakra will generally turn this rush off by itself when the danger has passed. If not, and your *kundalini* runs upward into your other chakras for more than a day or so, see the *Kundalini* Healing in the Troubleshooting Guide of *Rebuilding the Garden*.

If you are not in immediate trouble, your large first chakra may simply be opening to new levels of awareness. This is a very good sign, but because molest contracts wreak so much havoc in the first chakra, I will ask you to keep an eye on your large first chakra for now.

The first chakra energy is very brave, and even foolhardy sometimes, which is why it is so good at helping you survive. Your newly healed first chakra needs your guidance and leadership as it awakens from its molest nightmare. It may get a little better and suddenly think it can run a marathon, spiritually speaking. It may think it can heal your every issue and stay open and unguarded, because life is suddenly safe. Be aware that your current lifestyle and surroundings may not be healthy enough right now. Protect your powerful first chakra from the harm that may be in your environment (get your protective third chakra up and working, please).

Please bring the edges of your too-open first chakra in to the normal three-to-five-inch diameter. Your chakra may be open to a larger size out of habit only, especially if you are always poised for danger. Its size may also still be directed by your molest contracts. Burn them now and get your chakra back to size. Chakras open and close like camera shutters, if you need that visual help in your attempts to change their shape. You can even use your hands to gently push the edges of your chakra into a smaller circular shape.

A closed first chakra is a sign of a shutting down of the life energy, or, perhaps, an attempt to ignore it. Closed first chakras appear on people in great physical or emotional pain, not from being in basic survival *per se* (which would create a too-open first chakra), but from being in deep denial of their own life path or lessons.

If you have closed your first chakra because you'd like to have just about any life but your own, it's time to take a hold of yourself. Certainly, closing this chakra will pull you away from your own life, but only at great peril. I see this decision to close down a lot in metaphysical circles, especially in the joy-only ones. People want to have only positive feelings, which is impossible on this planet. In order to live the happy-addict's life, it is necessary to be ungrounded and out of the body. Unfortunately, ungrounded people's lives soon fall into chaos.

Without a conscious connection to your first chakra, you won't be grounded. You will be unsettled, disorganized, emotionally paralyzed or volatile, and unprotected. The joy you crave will soon eat up all your intent and energy. Your life will fall apart as you chase after one emotion at the expense of all others. You'll make nutty decisions and choices, and your true path, which you gave up as too difficult, will suddenly seem very appealing. Your path, you will soon realize, was created with your specific strengths and weaknesses in mind.

Getting your feet back onto your path is easy. You just have to re-open your first chakra, and let your real and normal emotions emerge. Staying on your path is hard sometimes, but all the skills in *Rebuilding the Garden* will help you to maintain a constant course. Get your feet back under you please, and stop distracting yourself from the very lessons and situations you chose to deal with before you were born. God sent you here to live your own life and learn your own lessons. Your first chakra knows this. Listen to it!

The closing of the first chakra can also signal an individual's denial of the necessity of straightforward, unemotional, orgasm-centered sexuality. Closing the first chakra may seem like a way to escape all of its issues, especially the sexual ones, but it doesn't work. Closing off and ignoring the first chakra disrupts the grounding and the rest of the chakra system.

I always tell people with any closed chakras that it is perfectly normal to have issues, but that closing the chakra associated with those issues will create a hundredfold more issues, problems, and difficulties.

It is very easy to have difficulties with sex, survival, and grounding while maintaining a healthy first chakra. Punishing our chakra system because we don't want to deal with certain aspects of our wholeness is silly. It is our responsibility to make sure that we aren't penalizing ourselves or our chakras just because our lives aren't perfect. Regardless of the issues at hand, it is always correct to keep the chakras in working order. If your first chakra is closed now, take note of it, but let it be. After you have read the rest of the chakra chapters, and you are ready to heal your chakra system, check in on it again. It may open on its own, now that it knows you are aware and willing to help.

If you have a closed first chakra right now, but are not in any dangerous or survival-based situation, another possibility is that your chakra is closed for repairs. In a healthy and balanced chakra system, chakras may close down for a little while in order to heal and divest themselves of bad habits or damaging energy contracts. During these times, the other chakras look out for the closed one, and let it take a little vacation.

You will recognize a first chakra vacation by the health and color of all the other chakras, by the absence of immediate survival issues, and by the fact that you can stay grounded even though your first chakra is closed.

If your first chakra is on vacation, congratulate yourself and all of your other chakras, and give each of them a hello gift. When one of your chakras can take a safe rest like this, it means you have achieved health and communication in the chakra system as a whole! Support your chakra system further by placing two Sentries directly in front and in back of your first chakra. These Sentries will guard and heal your first chakra, which will open back up as soon as it is ready, usually in less than a week.

If your first chakra does not open by the end of a week's time, ask it what is needed. Usually, your first chakra will require a better Sentry and aura boundary system, and perhaps a new grounding cord. It might even need its neighboring chakras to be healed first. Trust this basic chakra to tell you what it needs in order to open up again.

TRAITS OF A HEALTHY FIRST CHAKRA: When the first chakra is open to the right size, it will be defined and flowing with a freely moving, clear red energy. The grounding cord will be healthy and defined as well.

People with healthy first chakras will be grounded, certainly, but they will also be in touch with their body and their sexuality on a purely physical, unemotional level. They will know what is right for them in terms of food, shelter, and sex partners—without needing to emote or ruminate on the rightness of each decision. They will have a solid stance, a strong, balanced gait, an awareness of where they are, and where they left their car, their car keys, and their energy.

Such healthy first chakra people will also feel centered and powerful, able to handle any health concern that comes up, even if that means being "sick" for a while until their body clears out.

If people live from their first chakra only, they can be earthy and basic beyond belief. They won't have the tempering influence of their other six chakras to balance their physicality with their spirituality. We won't spend too much time discussing unbalanced people, though. We're working toward wholeness, right?

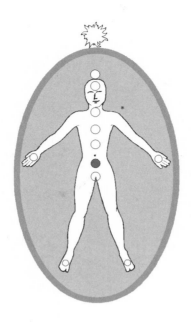

FURTHER INTO THE GARDEN

THE SECOND CHAKRA

This warm orange, receptive chakra sits just below the navel in the center of your body. The second chakra is the center of emotions, the musculature, gender identity, and sexuality beyond the first chakra's primal need to procreate.

The sexuality of the second chakra is one of connection, specific gender roles and identities, and the ability to bond and become one with a lover. The second chakra energy also allows us to bond in non-sexual situations and experience true body-level empathy. This is not always good, especially in interpersonal situations where clear boundaries are necessary for health.

In many cases molest survivors who are not connected to their first chakra because of the cording and programming there will over-identify with the energy of the second chakra. They will try to ground and center themselves there instead. This is a problem, because the second chakra exists to bond things together through emotion. In a healthy chakra system, this bonding can be used safely as but one of a number of relating skills. In an unhealthy system, a second chakra focus can create a person with very few emotional boundaries. This person, called a *clairsentient* (see the explanation below), will be bonded with everything and everyone around him.

The sexual energy of the second chakra is unhealthy if used all by itself as well. Second chakra-centered people will be deeply emotional lovers who require profound, to-the-dying-breath commitments from their partners. They will spend a huge amount of time seeking a transcendent, in-love feeling, as opposed to taking people as they are and loving them without so many superhuman requirements.

Trying to manage an adult sexual life from the second chakra alone can be emotionally exhausting for everyone concerned. It is best to get the first chakra up and running to create a balance between its hunka hunka burnin' love sexuality, and the second chakra's romantic ideals.

Because the second chakra is the center of gender identity, it is also strongly affected by molestation. All humans are supposed to maintain a psychological, emotional, physical, and spiritual balance of masculine and feminine energy, but many molest survivors cannot manage to do so. Gender and sexuality become unsafe and confused, and signs of imbalance are expressed in the functioning of the second chakra.

The second chakra reveals how much focused, expressive, masculine energy we allow in ourselves, in contrast to our diffuse, receptive, feminine energy. Generally, a person will skew away from the gender of their molester in their own personality, unless they feel that power resides in the molester's gender; in that case, they'll skew toward it. As in any other case of balance between two poles, a lack of balance in regard to gender is not an ideal state.

A good way to check in on your gender balance is to place two small reading roses just in front of your second chakra. On your left should be your feminine energy rose, and on your right, your masculine energy rose.

With these assignments made, let each rose become a symbol of its gender, and watch them both to see how they change, specifically in relation to one another. If one rose gets big and bright while the other goes dark and wilted, you've got yourself a pretty good gender skew going.

Study these roses, and go back to the chapter in *Rebuilding the Garden* on rose readings if you need a refresher on stem length and colors and so forth. Remember that these roses are an illustration of where your gender identity is right now. If these roses are very unhealthy and unbalanced, remind yourself that this is not a guarantee of a life-long gender imbalance. As is true of any other lingering damage from sexual assault, this gender imbalance can be examined, worked with, rehabilitated, and healed.

After you have read your primary gender-skew information, please thank and destroy your reading roses and place new, extremely healthy, grounded roses in their place. Dedicate these new roses to the healing of your gender skew. Endow them with health and protective abilities, groundedness, and beautiful colors.

These roses will act like little sentries as they stand guard in front of your very receptive second chakra. They will not only serve as healing place-holders for your masculine and feminine energy, but will also confront and ground out all the crazy societal messages about gender that infect our planet.

For excellent help in recognizing and honoring the differences between masculine and feminine energy, please read the books *He* and *She* by Robert A. Johnson. They're tiny books, but they are powerful!

A note about the second chakra: each chakra has a specific psychic ability attached to it, and this chakra's ability is rather tricky in a time as chaotic as ours. The second chakra heals and communicates through complete body-level empathy, or *clairsentience*.

With its clairsentient abilities, your second chakra can actually bring someone else's pain, emotions, or conflict inside you so you can feel it in your body. A good example of this kind of body-level empathy is when you double over in sympathy when you see someone else's testicles get kicked. You can actually feel it, even if you haven't got any testicles.

Being able to feel another's pain and to deeply understand their emotions and reactions is important. The problem with this depth of understanding lies in the fact that other people's energy will not and cannot work in our bodies. We do not have the ability to truly heal another's pain, because we do not have their tools.

Each person's pain is specific to them, and all pain comes with its own specific little tool set, as it were. I cannot heal your gender skew for you, but I can help you find the tools to heal it yourself. If I tried to pull your pain and confusion into my body, you would feel lighter for a while, but you wouldn't have learned your lesson. Your problem, or something very much like it, would soon come back. Plus, I would have your pain stuck in my second chakra, unless I was extremely conscientious about grounding it out.

Clairsentient healers who work from the second chakra are called *sponge healers*, and though they can perform miracles, they usually die of cancers and organ-wasting diseases. This is because their bodies cannot process that which is not theirs to heal. Their systems are simply overwhelmed by all the foreign energy they ingest. Though they may perform a fair number of healing miracles in their careers, the long-term costs are too high.

An example: my own borderline schizophrenia was created by my energy and my cells for a specific reason, and healing my own illness brought me to a new level of personal awareness. Though I required guidance, nutritional support, and information, the tools I needed to heal my own illness came with the illness. My ability to access those tools came from using my second chakra energy on myself.

By coming into direct empathic contact with my schizophrenic tendency, I was able to understand why it was manifesting in my body. When I saw the importance of the schizophrenia in protecting me from seeing or knowing the truth about my molestation, I was able to thank it and let it go. Instead of fighting and hating and drugging my disease, I was able, with the help of my own empathic abilities, to treat it as an ally in my healing.

My second chakra taught me that each imbalance exists for a specific, often protective reason. It taught me that the body in turmoil is not giving up, but trying its best to continue on in the face of trauma and hardship. When my schizophrenic tendencies showed me that they were a reaction to my molestation, I was able to heal that split, which released the need for any further insanity.

My schizophrenic tendencies served a very deep purpose for me on many levels, not the least of which was the imperative to no longer pretend everything was okay in my world. If I had given the responsibility of healing my psychiatric disturbances over to a healer of any kind, I could easily have ignored the message within my turmoil. If I had been healed miraculously by someone else, I would have experienced none of my own healing power. I also might have thought that the power to heal existed only in the miracle worker, and not in myself.

If I as a healer miraculously sponge someone else's mental illness off of them, I not only take away their opportunity to learn and move to new levels of personal power and awareness, but I place myself in unnecessary danger. Because I didn't create their mental illness, I don't have the tools to deal with their mental illness. I have no business bringing it into my body.

If I love people and want to be a real healer, I will allow them to have their own pain. I will help and guide them out of their misery, but I will not suck their misery into my body. If I love myself, I won't damage myself to prove that I'm a good healer. I can use the healing abilities of other chakras, or, in the best scenario, I can heal from all of them at the same time. In this way, I'll be able to understand another person's pain without having to become one with it.

Be aware of how open and receptive your second chakra is, because you can unconsciously sponge energy in any number of seemingly mundane situations. For instance, people who are very good at cleaning, organizing, or mucking out usually sponge up old energy with their second chakras as they scrape off grime or create a new filing system. Competent personnel managers or counselors generally sponge off the stress of others without realizing it.

Nurses are absolutely notorious sponge healers, as are massage therapists, court reporters, office managers, bookkeepers, parents, and humane society workers. The list goes on and on, and though women are more famous for sponging, men do it just as well and as often.

The best way to find out if you are a sponge healer is to examine your fatigue levels and the condition of your third chakra. If you are knocked out and exhausted at the end of a work week, if your stomach is constantly hurting, and you require long vacations far away from your home, you are probably sponging on a daily basis.

The exhaustion and the urge to get away from everything could be a sign of normal fatigue, but the stomach-ache in this instance signals that your protective third chakra is trying to get your attention. Your third chakra is trying to get you to protect both it and your second chakra, please. Also, the constant need for far-off vacations is a dead sponging giveaway. People with functioning psychic and emotional boundaries do not have to leave town to relax.

Your anti-sponging defense mechanism will be to place many grounded Sentries in front of your second and third chakras. Check in on their size and general health as often as you can. Remind yourself, over and over again, that you can exist and be important even when you don't fix everything and everyone around you.

Your sponging abilities are important, but only in a healthy, balanced, and aware energy body. If you've got sponging abilities that are far greater than your other intuitive abilities, you'll experience painful spiritual and physical imbalances.

Clairsentience is not all bad—don't misunderstand me. Clairsentience is an important healing ability within the self, and it is a vital part of a whole and healthy spiritual healing arsenal. By itself, though, sponging is safest and works best only between members of the same family, especially in the case of a parent-to-child healing relationship.

A mommy-or-daddy kiss on a cut or bruise has absolutely magical healing properties. The pain drains right out of injuries when parents kiss them. While children are under the age of thirteen, they are psychically connected to their parent's energy anyway, so this kind of parent-to-child sponging will have no ill effects for the parent.

Sponging between siblings or older children and parents or grandparents can also be done safely. The genetic and emotional material is similar enough for the body to process without too much damage or difficulty (except in incestuous families. Please see the chapter called *Special Topic: Cording*). This is really the only time I can recommend sponge healing on its own. Other situations are simply unsafe and unnecessary. People cannot learn their lessons if their difficulties are removed, hey-presto! And, healers will not survive if they insist on using sponge healing in non-family situations.

WARNING: If you have arrived at a place of understanding and forgiveness for your molester without ever really becoming angry, you most likely are cording into him or her from your second chakra. If you are feeling empathy for your molester's sad plight and ignoring your own feelings of betrayal, rage, terror, and hurt, you are still sponging. You are still bound up in a contract.

Clairsentients are very much at risk in relationships with manipulative and off-center people like abusers and molesters. Sponge healers have the requisite lack of boundaries that make abusers feel so welcome. A sponge healer's aura and chakra system say, in effect, "Come on in, the water's fine!" No protection there!

Sponge healers are often disconnected from their interior emotional reality. Because their second chakra, which is the center of emotions and emotional protection, is always busy with anything but their own needs, sponge healers really don't know how they feel. Their emotional confusion is such that one could abuse a sponge healer for years before they become aware of the abuse. Most people in a sponge healer's life depend on this fact.

This abuse is unfortunate, but it can be halted. Remember, sponging is a contractual agreement. Contracts can be rolled up and burnt as easily as they are written and entered into. Cords (see the chapter called *Special Topic: Cording*) to any chakra are also aspects of contractual agreements. These agreements can be grounded out, rolled up, and burnt. Just because spongers have spent a long time sponging doesn't mean they have to keep doing it. It is a habit that can be broken. In the case of sponging and cording into a molester, especially a molester from one's own family, it is a habit that *must* be broken.

Molested people who become out-of-balance clairsentients are so filled with other people's energy that they can't even find their own feelings anymore. In essence, their emotional energy is used up on other people's problems. This is the reason many sponge healers stay with their healing work, even though it starts to kill them. Sure, it hurts, but it also has the big payoff: they don't have to feel their own feelings! The pain *seems* to come from the present, and they can deal with that. The pain that sits inside them in the dark seems too big to handle. For these people, the dangers of sponging seem preferable to the terrors of their inner trauma.

If sponge healers can take the big leap of faith and trust, they can become aware of their own second chakra and its ability to channel emotional states that instruct and heal. In a surprisingly short amount of time, spongers who re-connect to the beauty and strength of their second chakras will soon become uninterested in sponging for others.

Healthy, balanced clairsentients will have so much fascinating information and healing energy available for themselves that they won't have to stick their second chakra into other people's healing process. They will be able to find the healing information their own emotions hold for them, and they will learn to connect and empathize with others in healthy, non-clinging ways.

Working with the second chakra is simple. You won't have to spend weeks worrying over it or begging it to heal. All that is required is awareness, and the willingness to change. When you get to the sections on readings and healings that follow these chakra descriptions, pay close attention to your wounded second chakra, but spend most of your time getting it back into alignment and contact with the rest of your chakra system. This balance, more than anything else, will heal your second chakra.

The overuse of the second chakra creates problems with grounding (the first chakra), psychic protection (the third chakra), self-love and body/spirit communication (the fourth chakra), and on up the line. Healing the second alone will help, but it is imperative to re-balance the entire chakra system and to pull each chakra into present time. Otherwise, the associated problems in the other chakras could throw the second chakra back into imbalance once again.

The healthiest chakra is one that is a working member of a functioning system. A second chakra problem requires not only your help, but the help of all your other healed chakras as well. Once you heal it and place it back into alignment and communication with your chakra system as a whole, your second chakra will receive help, support, and healing from all your other chakras, as well as from you.

OPEN OR CLOSED SECOND CHAKRA

A very wide-open second chakra in an unbalanced chakra system must be brought back to size (three to five inches in diameter) immediately. Since this chakra is so receptive and generally unprotected, it can draw foreign energy into your body before you are even aware that any energy was lurking around.

Re-size this chakra by imagining the closing mechanism of a camera shutter, or use your hands to re-form it. When you are new at closing off a life-long sponging tendency, it is very good to keep this chakra at least an inch smaller than the others. Cover it with strongly protective, grounded Sentries, front and back. After any period of non-family sponge-healing, the second chakra may need a long rest.

When closing a too-open second chakra, it is good to take a fast from needy or manipulative people for a while, and to seek out only those friends and family members who honor, understand, and value you. You may have difficulty finding such people if you have spent a long time as an unbalanced clairsentient, but there will usually be one or two caring individuals hidden away somewhere.

If anyone in your sphere has urged you to rest or take care of yourself, or offered you help and healing even though you always refuse, seek them out. Your second chakra and your overused clairsentient ability will require the support of another human being who knows how to give without giving everything away.

A wide-open second chakra in a healed and generally balanced chakra system is the sign of an emotional or sexual opening that is necessary before the next stage in growth can occur. The way to tell if your very-open second is healthy is by its color, which should be a very clear and warm orange without any other colors mixed in. If your other chakras, specifically the first and third, are also healthy, you can let this chakra remain large for as long as a week.

Place two strongly grounded Sentries in front and in back of your open second chakra (inside your aura) to protect it from moving backward into sponge healing, and keep an eye on it. It should get itself back to normal before a week is out. If it hasn't, please re-size it yourself.

A closed second chakra is a sign that either the emotions or the connective and emotive aspects of sexuality are turned off. The closed second chakra, along with a very open first chakra (a skew which creates an earthy, non-empathic, unemotional personality and sexuality), is a societally condoned position for men to take. If you're a man, or a woman who runs a heavily masculine gender skew, don't be surprised by this imbalance. It's not a tough skew to fix in the quiet solitude of your meditative moments, but the resulting level of emotional openness and empathy can be difficult to support out in the world.

If the people in your life have known you as a cold and unemotional person, they may see you as someone who just doesn't care. They may not confide in you, or include you in social events, which has probably been fine with you.

When you re-open your second chakra, it won't be fine anymore to be isolated. It will feel awful. You may experience anger, sadness, and all the childhood or adolescent emotions you stuffed when you decided to shut off your emotional link to other humans. Channel those emotions with the skills you learned in *Rebuilding the Garden*. Your emotions belong to you, and they can heal you.

In addition, seek out the people who never really let you become stone cold in their presence. There will always be one or two brave people who try or have tried to reach you emotionally. Stay away from the people who try to manipulate your emotions in order to pull a reaction from you. Instead, seek out those who have shared their emotions, or cried in front of you, even though you made it clear that you had no emotions to share. These people were never fooled by your emotionless state, and they will not be surprised or dismayed by your process of opening to your emotions.

Surrounding yourself with the protection of emotionally-supportive people will protect your second chakra in the world, just as the Sentries can protect it inside your aura. If you are careful to stay with other emotionally open people, the emotional vulnerability that comes with a newly opened second chakra will not be used against you.

People with healthy second chakras care about the world, their place in it, the feelings and lives of others, and the wisdom of their own reactions and emotions. As such, a too-open second chakra can be a real detriment in a dog-eat-dog environment.

The second chakra makes you care, and our society is a perfect example of what happens when no one really does. We're falling apart here, because people are too frightened to connect and feel. This makes room for all sorts of everyday crimes against humanity, not to mention that it creates the need for out-of-control, sponge-healing martyrs who die by the thousands without healing anyone, really, least of all themselves.

There are a million reasons to keep your second chakra closed, and to refuse to feel or connect in healthy ways. The only reason to open it is so that you can live as a fully human being, and not as a skew-filled reaction to the society around you.

The second chakra needs permission from you, not society, in order to open back up. Your second chakra belongs to you, as does your ability to feel, and your ability to connect. No one else, least of all a sick society, has any business forcing you to close down your natural abilities. If you don't believe me, ask your first chakra. It has no patience with such idiocy. If you let it, your first chakra energy will come up into your deadened second chakra and clear out all the cobwebs so you can open up your emotions once again.

One of the best ways to begin to work with and open your second chakra is to rely on water and fluidity. Hot baths and water therapy help relax the musculature, which in turn releases the skeleton, which in turn creates a more flexible, emotive and fluid walk, stance, and attitude.

Fluid movements and swaying dances are especially supportive of the second chakra. I find that the simple act of allowing the hips to sway when walking or moving will release the pent-up and static energy in the pelvis. This release in itself will help to open the second chakra.

Remember, it's okay to have issues with emotions or sexuality, but closing off your second chakra in response to those issues will adversely affect your energy system and the rest of your life. If you close off the energy center that houses your emotions and your gender sexuality, you will not move beyond your difficulties. How can you, when this basic life energy, healing ability, and information is unavailable to you? Trust me, you can have your emotional issues *and* a healthy second chakra. The two states are not mutually exclusive.

When you and your chakras are healthy, but your second is still closed, it can signal a second-chakra vacation.

All chakras shut down periodically for repairs when the system is strong enough to let them do so. If you've gone off sponging and are concentrating your healing, empathic energy on yourself, you can perform absolute healing miracles in your energy body.

When your chakra system gets to a point of strength, your previously overworked second chakra may go "off-line" in order to remove cords, old sponge-healer programming, and other signs of disease and imbalance. The other chakras will watch out for the second chakra during this time, and it will open back up when it is ready.

You can identify a second chakra vacation by the health of the other chakras, by the absence of your usual cast of needy hangers-on, and by the sense of flow and relaxation in your pelvis and muscular body, even though your second is closed for now.

To support your second chakra in its time off, you can place two grounded Sentries inside your aura, at the front and back of your second chakra. These will help to guard and heal your second chakra until it comes back into service, which should be in a matter of days, or a week at the most.

After a week's vacation, your second chakra should be ready to get back to work. If not, ask it why not, and listen to its answer. Often, it will need a more vital aura or Sentry system to protect it from unconscious clairsentience. It may also need you to heal your protective third chakra. Give it your support.

As with any healthy chakra vacation, thank all your chakras for being well and aware enough to allow your second chakra a rest. Give them each a hello gift. They are doing a fabulous job.

TRAITS OF A HEALTHY SECOND CHAKRA: When the second chakra is open and flowing with a healthy, clear, warm orange energy, the body has a peaceful and sensual fluidity to add to the centered groundedness of the first chakra. A healthy second chakra confers an emotive, responsive connection to nature, to animals and humans, to the self, and to the spirit world.

A healthy gender balance creates deeply nurturing, focused, and capable people who are also spiritually aware and emotionally responsive. People with healthy second chakras have a fluid, languid walk, like felines, and a very deep understanding of the flow of events and people around them. By connecting to their own emotions, they connect to the world.

Healthy second chakras also supply a level of internal healing that is powerful beyond belief. When the total empathy of the second chakra is brought to bear on illnesses, it can get to the emotional root that brought about the illness in the first place.

By using the second chakra's clairsentient ability inside their own body, healthy clairsentients can speak to cancer cells, viruses, tissues, and diseases on their own primal level and ask them why they are living (or dying) in the body. The emotive and foundational answer each disease offers is always fascinating. Once it is understood and honored at this basic, feeling level, real healing of bodily dis-ease can occur.

Though the emotions have long been considered "lower" than the intellect, people with a healthy connection to their second chakras and their own emotions are wise beyond mere mental knowledge. They know *why* facts are true or false, not just that the facts exist. Connection to the emotional realities makes intellectual realities *meaningful*, not just factual.

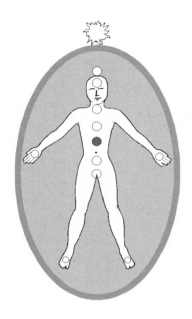

FURTHER INTO THE GARDEN

THE THIRD CHAKRA
(OR SOLAR PLEXUS)

This sunny yellow, expressive chakra sits right in the center of the solar plexus, directly between the navel and the sternum.

The third chakra is involved in thought and intellect, and with the effect of thought on the body (your susceptibility to psychosomatic illness). It is also the center of the psychic immune system. The third chakra will react to psychic danger by closing down, turning on very hot, or by spreading its energy out to protect its neighbors (the receptive fourth and second chakras) from harm.

A gnawing stomach-ache that is not connected to hunger is often the sign of your third chakra trying to close in the face of dangerous people or energy in your environment. The third chakra will also try to close, or open far too wide, when your Sentry and aura are too dainty and ornamental to do any real work in protecting your personal territory. Beef them up!

The third chakra is the uppermost body-level chakra. There are three body-level chakras (the first through the third), three spirit level chakras (the fifth through the seventh), and one transitional chakra (the fourth, which acts as a bridge between the spirit and the body). The eighth chakra, or the Gold Sun, is the overseeing chakra.

As the topmost body-level chakra, the third chakra is responsible for filtering spiritual information down to the first and second chakras. This filtering and passing on of information from spirit is what keeps the bodily aspects of the body/spirit connection healthy and alive.

When the third chakra and the heart chakra are healthy, the third will accept and translate the information coming down from the three spirit chakras through the heart. The third chakra will then pass this translated information along to the second and first chakras.

If your fourth chakra is unbalanced and the information coming down from it is not clear, your third chakra may spend all its time translating garbled messages. The receipt of gibberish from an unhealthy or overused fourth chakra can leave your third chakra and you open to attack. The translation process takes your third chakra's energy and attention away from the identification of foreign energy in your environment.

Your hard-working third chakra may try to keep your body/spirit connection alive and healthy, even if your fourth chakra is not able to offer clear information. However, if your overworked third chakra doesn't have the time and energy to keep up with its other main job, which is to keep you safe and protected, you may leave your body anyway.

If your third chakra is unhealthy (an example would be if you choose to stay in a dangerous relationship that forces your third chakra to remain eternally, exhaustingly vigilant), it may have to ignore all the spiritual information coming from your fourth chakra. It may have to work overtime just to keep you safe. You won't be living—you'll only be surviving. Soon, because your normal fourth-to-third chakra communication is blocked, you will have yet another body/spirit split.

The third chakra is also responsible for gathering and sending body-chakra information to the spirit chakras by way of the heart chakra. When this exchange is happening as it should, the spirit-level information and abilities of the upper chakras tend to pertain to more rational, real-world details. A good example of a working exchange of spirit/body information would be clairvoyance that relates to your own present-day reality, and spiritual information that tells you about that crick in your neck, or a food that is causing you trouble.

If the third chakra is gummed up and can't channel body-level information to the upper chakras, the upper chakra's information will be unreadable in the body. Either that, or the information will pertain to goofy things like the political situation in Manila (when you are not, and do not even know a Philippine national), or the knowledge of a plane crash about which you can do nothing.

Without the support of the third chakra and the realities of the body, the upper chakras can become ungrounded, and bring in all sorts of unrelated material. The fourth chakra might open too wide and pour all its energy away. The fifth might pick up voices from all over. The sixth might see unrelated, unusable visions, and the seventh might channel the information of unhelpful or unaware spirits who have no real connection to your life. Maintaining a healthy third-fourth connection will put a stop to all that silliness.

As with a number of aspects of spirituality that have been hopelessly confused here in the West, the third chakra has been unnecessarily singled out as a less-than-perfect chakra. I really don't understand why this thought form has become so prevalent, but the story is that the best chakra to have is the fourth (or the "heart-love" chakra). Apparently, the bad "power" chakra, which is the third, keeps people out of their hearts and stuck in worldly power.

It seems that the third chakra is responsible for wars, racism, money, egotism, the I.R.S., and clog-dancing. Or something like that. When we get to the section on the fourth chakra, I am going to have a little tantrum about the damage this crazy one-chakra idea has created for the poor heart chakra, but I'd also like to stand up for the beleaguered third chakra right now.

The only truly healthy chakra is one that is an aware, communicative member of a living, working chakra system. We've seen what can happen when the first chakra is played with and invited to blast upward into the other chakras for fun. It creates imbalance, disruptions, and an overall lack of health and useful awareness.

An imbalance will also be created by shutting any one chakra down, which is what many people do when they hear that the third, or "power" chakra is the root of evil. These people are taught that the empathic, loving heart chakra attitude is the only attitude to have, and that the wacky idea of allowing the third chakra to do its work of protection, separation, and immunity would destroy the whole love-in experience.

Yeesh. I'm here to tell you that this is completely untrue. The third chakra simply *is*. It is not good or evil, right or wrong! The third chakra performs dozens of vital functions, including the management of the entire immune system. The function that has given the third chakra a bad rap is the one that allows it to control any incoming energy.

If your third chakra senses a fight with another person, (and you are not aware of your energy yet) it may allow you to throw a controlling energy cord (see the chapter called *Special Topic: Cording*) to that person's third chakra so that you can get an upper hand in the ensuing melee. Sometimes this cord will stop attackers in their tracks, and you may begin to rely on third chakra cording to get your way with people, as it were.

This is the extent of badness you can commit with the third chakra. As with any cording, it is a badness that can be unlearned. Turning off the entire third chakra just because it's possible to cord with it is extremely foolish (besides, *all* chakras can throw cords, even the celebrated heart chakra!). Without the vigilant protection system of a functioning third chakra, both the fourth and the second chakra are liable to fall into damaging sponging habits of all kinds.

Without the communicative aspects of a functioning third chakra, a mind/spirit/body schism is nearly assured. The upshot is: don't listen to all the hooey about the bad third "power" chakra and close it down to fit in with some current ideal. Your power to protect your own energy system is absolutely irreplaceable in a healthy whole life, no matter what the current trends are in New Age thought.

A healthy third chakra is actually vital to the functioning of the heart-love fourth chakra. If the protective and communicative third chakra is turned off, the heart chakra will eventually become very large and unhealthy. All the love the heart contains will pour away until its owner has none left for anyone.

This unfortunate occurrence can be seen regularly in heart-love healers who burn out by the thousands as their bodies break down and their energy dissipates. Their own healing will commence when they turn their protective and energetic third chakra back on and begin to live whole lives again.

We can circumnavigate this whole, sad burn-out process by keeping our third chakras healthy, open, and included in our whole lives. Third chakra cording will cease in a connected and aware chakra system. When the clairvoyant sixth chakra is working and overseeing the energies around it, the sixth will alert the third chakra of any upcoming danger. The third chakra in a healthy system will then strengthen (or ask you to strengthen) its aura, grounding, and Sentry, so that damage, and unconscious cording, is less likely.

In the physical world, there are dangers. Our bodies are spectacularly unprotected in mammalian terms. We have no claws or horns or musk glands or sharp teeth. We don't even have a protective covering. Our bodies have to deal with this every day. If we fall into a pattern of New Age thought that sees all energy and all human encounters as safe, we shut off our third chakras, and then have no protection whatsoever. None.

Without protection, we become less, not more useful in the world, because our third chakras not only protect us, but define us and our place in its healing. Without the third chakra's self-protective support, we become less than ourselves.

In the physical immune system, the identification of foreign bodies and foreign foods is not just a process of alarm and defense. In order to identify foreign agents, the immune system must know what its own cells look like. The immune system essentially goes through the body in each moment, saying, "This is mine, that's mine, that's mine, this here is mine...."

The immune system can only identify a foreign or invading substance ("That is NOT mine!") if it knows itself. In the healthy immune system, self-preservation comes from self-knowledge. In an imbalanced immune system, the body's defenses are often used against a person's own healthy tissues, because the immune agents don't know what is theirs, and what is not theirs.

The same principle holds true in the spiritual immune system. In a healthy, self-aware person, the third chakra energy moves through the aura and chakra system, constantly touching and monitoring the energies within, saying, "This emotion is mine, that energy is mine, this intuition is mine,..." until it comes upon a foreign substance. When it does, it alerts the sixth chakra, which studies and categorizes the energy; or it alerts the second chakra, which performs an energy-matching with the strange energy to determine its emotional content.

The healthy third chakra then alerts its owner with a stomach twinge, or a shimmering in the aura. Hopefully, its owner will respond. If not, the healthy third will wrap the foreign energy in a cocoon, and wait until the next healing session, when the energy will be found and grounded out.

In the unhealthy chakra system, especially where a body/spirit split has occurred, or the all-accepting mind-set is present, the third chakra will be so harried and overworked that it will often just smack all people away, or cord into them in order to gain some sort of control. In many instances, this third chakra's alerting stomach twinges (usually ignored) will turn into full scale digestive disturbances, ulcers, or hiatus hernias.

In such an unhealthy system, you will also find a person with very little useful self-awareness. Their third chakra, which is so degraded and damaged by their split state or all-accepting nature, will have no time at all to identify what belongs to it. This third will spend its time putting out fires, trying and failing to connect to the often runaway-healing heart chakra above it, or wondering when the next *kundalini* blast will hit. This psychic immune system will experience an auto-immune illness. It will begin attacking its own unrecognized energy.

Such people will have a hard time making decisions or remembering things. They will be ungrounded and unsafe, they will often be far off-path, and they will be filled with a quiet despair that all their all-accepting philosophy will not cure. Eventually, they will become spiritually and physically ill, as would anyone with a non-functioning immune system.

Healing for these people generally arrives in the form of fits of anger and rage. Anger, as you know, contains boundary energy. Anger also loudly proclaims the existence of many unmet and ignored personal needs. When anger is channelled, and the underlying emotions of despair, depression, and fear are given their due as well, the third chakra will often come back on line.

When the third chakra is back in business, it will ask you to close down your heart chakra for a while. It will ask you to become aware of and responsible for your authentic human emotions ("this is mine"). With these supports, you will be able to ground and center yourself within your own life, and learn to integrate your chakra energies with one another.

When your energies are available to you, and your third chakra is healthy, self-protective, and self-aware, you will no longer rely on the crutch of accepting everything outside of you *instead* of learning to accept everything inside.

Going outside of yourself to find inner peace is backward. It is also a diversion. Don't divert. Get your third chakra up and running, and it will teach you to accept the most important person in the world: yourself.

Self-accepting people accept others, within reason. All-encompassing, other-accepting people have no reason or rationale, and soon cannot accept themselves or their own reactions. Other-accepting people become runaway, out-of-control healers who are soon enough incapacitated and unable to help or heal anyone. Self-accepting people maintain their spiritual health, and can easily help others, when they deem that help to be necessary.

OPEN OR CLOSED THIRD CHAKRA

A very wide-open third chakra needs to be re-sized immediately. If the nearby chakras are shut down or strangely colored, or the openness of the third chakra is accompanied by stomach, kidney, or mid-back pain, it is a sign of general chakra system distress, danger in your daily environment, or cording problems.

Closing down and protecting your too-open third chakra with Sentries and negativity-eating gift symbols is very important, but so is continuing on and healing the rest of your chakra system as soon as possible.

Because the third chakra is a center of immunity and the ability to be safely separate on an energy level, it can be affected by assaults or imbalances in any of the other chakras. A third chakra in distress requires immediate attention so that the rest of the chakras and the aura can function normally. The sections on chakra readings and healings that follow these descriptions will guide you through a chakra balancing meditation.

A very open third chakra in an otherwise healthy and aligned chakra system is a sign that the spirit and body are communicating, and that the third is gathering energy and information in order to make a leap in the conscious aspects of thought and health. However, many supposedly healthy spiritual people's open third chakras are not healthy at all.

You can identify a healthy open third chakra by the health and color of *all* your other chakras (not just the ones nearby), and by a feeling of safety and peace in your exterior environment, and in your digestive tract. A chaotic exterior or interior environment signals that this opening is not a healthy leap in consciousness, but an unhealthy use of the third chakra.

Pro-heart-chakra/anti-third-chakra teachings suggest to open to all energy because we are all *one*. This often leads people to open their third chakras very wide, often until its edges reach the very edge of the body. Such teachings exhort one to become non-judgmental, non-discerning, and accepting of all energy, all experience, all people, and all circumstances. Such teachings *require* an unhealthy third chakra.

In spirit, we are all one. There is no work to be done to achieve a state of oneness in spirit. At the spirit level, we are all God's children, coming from the same place, though we will always have our individual spiritual messages to process. Spiritual oneness does not require an unhealthy third chakra; therefore, spiritual oneness will have no damaging side-effects.

In the intellectual realm, we can do a bit of work to become one. We can change our thoughts, or expand our intellect to embrace all forms of thought. At the intellectual level, we can learn to come from the same place, though our mental process will always be individual. Intellectual oneness does not require an unhealthy third chakra either, and besides a bit of confusion or petulance when long-cherished beliefs are shown to be insupportable, intellectual oneness will have no damaging effects.

In the emotional realm, it's pretty easy to become one with others. Your second chakra can open and allow another person's emotive state to come right into your body. This is not a perfect situation, because it relies on the bad psychic habit of sponging, but it can be done.

A better method of working with another's emotions is to honor and validate them from within your own separate, individual emotional reality. Maintaining a separate reality (which is the opposite of sponging) is easy when you have a healthy third chakra.

Emotional oneness requires sponging, which requires the dropping of boundaries, the acceptance of foreign energy, and a lack of psychic protection. Emotional oneness *requires* an unhealthy third chakra.

The damage seen in a person who attempts emotional oneness is complicated. Not only will all the troubles related to second chakra damage be present, but physical damage may be present as well, due to the prerequisite imbalance in the third chakra.

Such emotionally-one people will have a very low immunity, both to the emotions of those around them, and to opportunistic infections of the body. They will suffer from recurrent colds and flus, allergies, food and chemical sensitivities, stomach and digestive problems, and trouble sorting their thoughts and reactions from the thoughts and reactions of those nearby.

When emotional oneness (sponging) is attempted outside of the family sphere, and foreign energy is courted and drawn into the body, the third chakra *must* be damaged in the process.

Physical oneness is an impossibility. There is no way to become one and stay one with someone on a physical level. Sexuality can bond lovers for an instant, but only an instant. Longer contact is both inappropriate and ridiculous. Bodies cannot become one with other bodies.

The only person we must become one with is ourselves. The only spirit we must become one with is God. Anything else is a diversion.

Our molesters, by trying to force us into an emotional and physical oneness with them, showed each of us a pretty clear picture of where such diversions can lead.

Don't divert. Get back to the real work of becoming one with yourself, and one with your concept of God. When you know yourself, you will know all people. Trying to know all people *instead* of yourself is backward.

When you know God, you will know everything you need to know. Gathering all experience and information in order to know God is backward too. Your healthy, working third chakra will remind you of this again and again if you will just listen to it.

By reminding you of your individual goals, thoughts, tasks, reactions, emotions, health concerns, and realities, your healthy third chakra will make true and useful oneness possible by protecting you from oneness that is unworkable, unnecessary, and insupportable.

If your third chakra is wide open in a healthy, balanced chakra system, and you experience *none* of the symptoms of emotional oneness above, you may congratulate your chakra system on its health and awareness.

It is very unusual in this day for a third chakra to be too open because it is healthy enough to move on to the next level of awareness. Our society, and numerous religious and spiritual teachings, degrade the third chakra's protective aspects to such an extent that I am surprised when one works at all in early readings!

Please protect and honor your healthy chakra system by placing a congratulatory hello gift in front of each of your chakras. Also, please place at least three strongly grounded Sentries at the front and back of your open third chakra (inside your aura) as a protection against any wandering foreign energy.

Carefully monitor your open third chakra, and use your hands to close it back down to its regular three-to-five inch diameter at the end of one week. It may want to stay wide open for a longer period of time. If your environment is safe and sane enough, let it stay open. If not, close it down a little and get yourself to a sane environment before you allow your third chakra to open back up again. In such a safe place, your third chakra, and all your other chakras, will be able to do their best work.

A constantly closed third chakra can be a sign of a person's unwillingness to think about or question the life she is living. It can also mean that she is not willing or able to protect herself in the face of danger.

Molest survivors who are still drawn to molesting or abusive environments in their adult lives usually have a very small or closed third chakra. Opening the third can be very distressing for these people. When it is working, a healthy third chakra will want to get the hell away from the everyday dangers many molest survivors think they need in order to feel normal and alive.

A working third chakra asks you to think about safety, right livelihood, correct thinking patterns, warm and healing environments, and peace. These are wonderful topics, unless your current life choices steer you away from all five. In opening your third chakra, you will have to ask the hard questions. Is your life safe? Are you supported and cared for? If not, why not?

Your newly opened third chakra will react to dangers in your environment. If it has been closed for a long time, and your environment is completely unsafe, your third chakra may go a little crazy with stomach distress, fears, rages, rescue scenarios, racing thoughts, and more.

Please support your third chakra by moving away from your abusive patterns. Blame other people all you like, but get yourself out. Use all the skills you have, reach out to all the supports you can find, but *get out*. Your health *requires* you to live as a free person. Your healthy third chakra will help you protect yourself long enough to get to freedom.

When I re-opened my third chakra after a fifteen-year closure, I had so much work to do to regain my life that I felt overwhelmed. It took fully six years of work, processing, and help to get all the way back to health, but only one minute to take back my control and regain my freedom. My freedom came back as soon as I opened my third chakra and began to protect myself.

My immediate freedom required the support of a battered women's shelter, a rape crisis group, the welfare system, and my return to school after a ten-year absence. Your freedom may require less support. Let's hope so.

However far you may seem to be from your freedom, you are in actuality only a moment away. Re-open your third chakra, and you'll see what I mean.

When a normally healthy third chakra closes suddenly, and all the other chakras are working and balanced, it can mean that the third chakra is reacting to a controlling person or energy pattern in the immediate environment by becoming unavailable for cording.

This kind of immediate closing in a healthy third chakra is often accompanied by a hunger pang or minor, fleeting stomach distress. Be aware of these moments of clear communication from your working third chakra, and assist it by turning the front of your body away from the offending energy. This will make cording more difficult, and it will give you a minute to put up a Sentry blanket, do an Aura Stomp, or burn some contracts (see *Rebuilding the Garden*).

Make sure that you give free hello gifts to the person or energy pattern that shows you, by trying to cord into your chakras, where your defenses are still in need of work. Thank them. They've done you a service.

A temporarily closed third in a healthy system can be a sign that a bit of quiet study is going on. Chakras sometimes go off-line for a little while when your awareness reaches a point of balance. They heal themselves, recharge their batteries, and get rid of cords while the other chakras watch out for them.

If you find a closed third chakra in an otherwise healthy system, and there is no identifiable danger in your immediate environment, you may be experiencing a third chakra vacation. You can identify this state by not only the health and condition of your other chakras, but by a sense of relaxation and well-being in your mid-back and your digestive tract, even though your third chakra is shut down.

Congratulate all your chakras for their excellent work, and give each of them a hello gift. Also, place two protective Sentries inside your aura, right in front and in back of your third chakra, and go on with your reading. Your third chakra should open back up on its own within a matter of days, or a week at the most. If not, ask it what help it would need from you in order to open up again. It will usually ask for a brighter aura boundary and a beefier Sentry system, or more awareness of your honest emotional responses to your life.

TRAITS OF A HEALTHY THIRD CHAKRA: When the third chakra is open and flowing with a clear, sunny yellow energy, it confers a centered intelligence to the body and the spirit. When it is part of a healthy lower chakra system, a working third chakra adds the ability to think, discern, process, and protect to the emotive and connecting qualities of the second chakra.

The healthy third chakra also lends an ability to protect the health through work, study, meditation, and application, in addition to the first chakra's purely physical, life-force type of healing and body maintenance. A healer with a healthy third chakra will have a virtual encyclopedia of information available to their clients, because true third chakra healing is supported by knowledge *and* faith.

A healthy and communicative third chakra also makes itself known through an all-over sense of comfort about spiritual knowledge and psychic abilities. When the third chakra is sending and receiving chakra system information freely, the body understands the spirit, and the spirit understands the body. Clairvoyant knowledge is real, valid, and useful, instead of confusing, unconnected, and ungrounded. Bodily information is heard, validated, and translated for spiritual help without mental obstruction. Self-knowledge is a simple, everyday reality for healthy third-chakra people.

A person with a working third chakra has achieved a balance between intellect, spiritual understanding, and bodily knowledge. These three aspects don't fight one another for dominance; instead, they communicate with and rely on one another. Add a healthy second chakra with its command of the emotions, and you've got a balanced quaternity—all four sides of a perfect square.

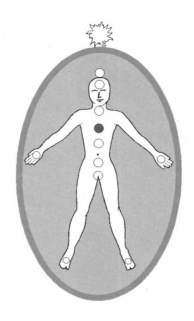

THE FOURTH
(OR HEART) CHAKRA

The fourth chakra is a light emerald green, receptive energy center that resides in the center of the chest. It is called the heart chakra, but it is not centered over the physical heart as much as it is over the sternum.

Oh, the heart chakra ... the celebrated, courted, deified, overworked, misunderstood heart chakra. This energy center has had so much said and written about it that it's hard not to get crushed under all the weighty suppositions, or imprisoned along with it in the temple of ritual and superstition created by so many *old souls* and *higher beings*. Bleah. Let's start over from scratch, shall we?

The heart chakra is a light emerald green, receptive energy center that is involved with the ability to love and feel compassion, both for oneself, and the world outside. The heart chakra should be connected to the hand chakras. If this connection is not healthy, the ability to give, love, connect, and receive may be damaged. In any study or healing of the heart chakra, the hand chakras must be included. This connection is vital in the chakra healing techniques that follow. Please study the hands and their connection to the heart in the chapter on hand chakras later in this book.

The heart chakra is the central, or transitional chakra, which means that it bridges the gap between the three body chakras below it, and the three spirit chakras above. In a healthy system, the heart chakra accepts the purely spiritual information of the upper chakras (which is gathered by and sent directly from the fifth, or throat chakra) and translates it into the language of the lower chakras. The heart chakra also translates the purely physical information of the lower chakras (which is gathered by and sent directly from the third chakra) and translates it into language the upper three chakras can understand.

Because of its vital linking responsibilities, the health of the fourth chakra is paramount for anyone wishing to heal a spirit/body split. When the fourth chakra is up and running, it works as an information collection and distribution center. It constantly facilitates and mediates between the spirit and the body. Without the support of a fit and capable heart chakra, the spirit and body tend to career off onto all sorts of mutually exclusive tangents.

So, given the above information, you'd think that people involved in spiritual study would have a leg up on normal folks in regard to the heart chakra. Think again!

Unfortunately, students in most spiritual growth and meditation classes often have the most damaged, overburdened, non-functional heart chakras imaginable. This is because so much

THE FOURTH CHAKRA 53

emphasis is placed on the heart's ability to love others that all of its diverse and intrinsically useful auxiliary functions are essentially ignored.

Loving and forgiving others is considered the best possible spiritual behavior. Giving selflessly and compassionately is also thought to be a supreme function. These are some of the leading traits of fourth chakra energy. They are also some of the leading traits of de-selfed, dissociated, runaway healers if they are not in balance with the leading traits of the other six central chakras.

Yes, loving others is vital—it's irreplaceable—but such other-love is not to be used as an excuse to de-self in the early portions of a spiritual journey. Truly loving others comes after learning to love the whole self: the creepy, majestic, childish, exquisite, stupid, all-knowing self. This doesn't happen if all the heart energy is directed outward and none is available for the self, or for communication between spirit and body.

All the other-love and other-compassion in the universe will lead nowhere if no love or compassion is directed inward. It's that simple. The heart chakra energy must be brought back into the body and honored before it can offer real love to others.

Over-emphasis on the heart chakra has many drawbacks. It destroys the balance and alignment of the chakra system as a whole, because the constant outpouring of heart energy leaves little energy for communication between the spirit chakras and the body chakras.

Over-emphasis on the heart chakra also interferes with psychic and physical immunity, because the third chakra usually spends too much time trying to protect the exhausted heart, and not enough time protecting the physical and energetic bodies.

An outpouring heart chakra also fosters an unwillingness to communicate and ask for help and healing. Because the communicative fifth chakra in this system is as overburdened as the third chakra, it can't help to express the needs of the individual.

Heart chakra people find themselves, again and again, healing in dangerous environments, completely unable to ask for support. Usually, they burn out, and then they can't help anyone, including themselves.

Overemphasis on the attributes of the fourth chakra can also damage the chakra itself. In most cases of overuse, the fourth chakra spreads out from its healthy circular shape into a hyper-extended oblong, reaching almost to the arms in unprotected healers, physicians, and therapists. These damaged heart chakras usually attract and nurture cording in order to survive (cording is an undeveloped method of spiritual communication and a special topic at the end of this book). Many damaged heart chakras end up looking like virtual cording switchboards.

One key sign of heart chakra problems is a contention or split between spirit and body. Because the heart is neither a body chakra nor a spirit chakra, people trying to live only from the heart cannot live in body *or* spirit. Living from the heart chakra *assures* a spirit/body split, because the heart chakra itself is in the ether between the spirit and the body.

Heart chakra healers will often vacillate widely between purely physical needs and pursuits, and purely spiritual beliefs and actions—and neither side will feel right. There will be no flow, and no balance between the two.

The owner of an overworked heart chakra will swing between loving and understanding all beings, and stuffing his face with chocolate while having tantrums about money. He will think that either he can meet his own needs and take from everyone else, or be totally selfless and give every part of himself away. There will be only black and white, with no communicative gray material in between.

People who try to live from the heart chakra alone will see life on this planet as *either/or*. *Either* they can live in the body and deal with ego, sex and money, *or* they can live from spirit, need nothing, and become totally selfless. They swing from one extreme back to the other without ever coming to the balance between the two poles.

I use a pendulum analogy with such people: a pendulum that is all the way to one side of its swing requires extreme energy in order to remain there. Something would actually have to grasp and hold a pendulum in place in order to keep it at one side or the other. This is totally unnatural. Pendulums only swing widely if one puts energy into them. In their natural state, pendulums move in a gentle, circular sway around the very center of their swing radius. Real pendulums live *only* in the gray matter between the black and the white.

The antidote to extreme and unnatural swings, of course, is balance. That balance is possible even in cases of grievous heart chakra damage.

Through balancing the chakra system, we can learn to love and heal appropriately, just as we can learn to emote, think, protect, survive, communicate, know, give, and receive appropriately.

If you are a heart chakra healer and find yourself unable to give to yourself, you will need to go through Part I of *Rebuilding the Garden* again in its entirety. When you have your basic spiritual separation and communication skills under you, you will benefit from the chakra healing and reading techniques that follow.

Keep the pendulum analogy in mind, though, to remind yourself that life on this planet is not either/or. We are spirits in bodies, and bodies full of spirit. Neither side is any better or worse than the other.

If you feel split in two by the needs of body and the needs of spirit, it's clear: your heart chakra isn't free to do its mediation and translation work within your chakra system. Burn your contracts with the wide pendulum swings, and use the freed-up energy to heal your heart instead. Read on.

OPEN OR CLOSED FOURTH CHAKRA

In any heart chakra difficulty, the hand chakras may also be involved. As you heal your heart chakra issues, please be aware of the connection between your heart and hands. Healing this connection will help to support any heart work you do. Please see the chapter on the hand chakras later in this book if your heart is in need of attention.

We've already talked about the reasons for and dangers of a very open or misshapen heart chakra. If the heart is wide open (larger than five inches in diameter) and other chakras are out of whack, get them all healed and back into alignment as soon as you can. Make sure your heart chakra and all your other chakras stay open to a three-to-five inch diameter at the very most.

A momentarily open heart chakra, as with any other chakra, is fine in an otherwise healthy and balanced chakra system. Heart chakras will open on their own when they need to move through issues relating to love, self-love, and competent spirit/body communication.

If your other chakras are balanced, and your upper back and lung area are free of discomfort, let your heart chakra remain wide open. Cover it, back and front, with a few Sentries of its own so it can work in peace and privacy. Check on it twice a day, but close it yourself (with your hands, or by imagining the closing of a camera shutter) if it remains wide open for longer than a week.

A misshapen heart chakra is another story. No matter how well the other chakras seem to be, a non-circular heart chakra is not a good thing.

This chakric shape-shifting can be a sign of cording, a tendency toward full-blown, out-of-control heart-chakra healing, or an attempt to reach out and replace self-love with the love and approval of others.

Please re-shape a non-circular heart chakra as soon as you find it. Use your hands to bring all the energy back in to a circular form, and skip forward to the chapter on the hand chakras for more support.

A tiny or tightly closed heart chakra is a sign of heart fatigue, betrayal of the heart, or distrust. Though it seems to be a protective move, the closing of the heart is self-punishing and other-punishing in actuality.

The heart that closes in response to heartbreak is a heart that agrees it is unlovable. It does not have the background of love or trust to weather the storms of human encounters. It does not believe in fairy tales, it cannot wish for happiness, and it cannot ask for love. It also cannot give love.

In addition, the closed heart stops all forward growth, because it refuses to act as a mediator between the spirit chakras and the body chakras. The closed heart creates more tragedy than it alleviates.

Re-opening the heart chakra is as difficult as it is imperative. The requirements are not only an almost foolhardy bravery, but a willingness to let go of long-cherished beliefs about lovelessness. Love exists everywhere, but one has to believe in love before it can be seen or felt.

All the slathering devotion in the world, and forty perfect relationships in a row, will mean nothing if the heart and the eyes are closed to love. If both are open, love appears in startling places … in the touch of a child at the supermarket, in the eyes of a neighborhood dog, in the dressing-down from a superior at work, and in the constant interruptions of a family member. Love is a language that requires special awareness; otherwise, it can sound like garbled noise that has no meaning.

When I am tempted to close my heart, I have a saying I go back to, which is from the book *Love is Letting Go of Fear*, by Gerald Jampolsky: "Love is constant; only the names change."

If I sit and think, I see that love of some kind was always available, and is always available. My problem is in craving only romance or undying excitement. I convince myself that there is no love, when in reality, the love available is just uninteresting to me. In those moments of closed-hearted stubbornness, I see that I am listening to love in my language, instead of listening to the language of love.

Love always provides itself, free for the taking, to people whose fourth chakras are open. All it requires is that the love be *used*, on the self or for others. Love must not be hoarded or hidden. Love requires your fourth chakra to stay open for the giving and receiving of love.

You can have numerous love, healing, and spirit/body communication issues rumbling around inside you, but you must keep your heart chakra healthy and open if you are ever to move on. Your open heart does not require you to love, heal, trust, or share anything; however, it must be open if you are going to live a whole life. Go ahead and be as unloving and unlovable as you like, but keep your fourth chakra open and healthy, okay?

If your chakra system is healthy and your heart is closed down right now, it may have gone off-line for repairs or study. Heart chakras are very susceptible to cording, and sometimes they need to sneak off and take a private vacation.

If you are able to stay in your body, and your upper back is flexible and unrestricted, your closed fourth chakra is not a problem. Congratulate your chakra system for being aware enough to perform its own healing, and give each of your other chakras a hello gift.

Also, please protect the back and front of your fourth chakra with at least four specifically dedicated Sentries. These Sentries will help your heart to maintain its privacy until it is ready to open up again—which should be in a matter of a few days, or a week at the most. Also, please be aware of the cording you allow in your heart, and do your best to break the cord habit. A special cord-removal process is included at the end of this book.

If your heart chakra is still closed after a week, it may need you to strengthen your aura boundary and Sentry system. It may also need you to heal its neighboring chakras so that its mediation work will be easier. Ask your heart what it needs. It will tell you.

TRAITS OF A HEALTHY FOURTH CHAKRA: A fully functional heart chakra in a balanced chakra system is a beautiful sight. The healthy heart channels love and acceptance inside the body and out into the world, and the emerald green energy inside it flows and moves with grace and fluidity.

The healthy fourth chakra is available to receive energy and information from the body and the protective third chakra, which it then invests with love and empathy before sending the information on to the upper chakras. The heart also heeds and accepts energy and information from the spirit and the communicative fifth chakra, and adds compassion and emotion to it before passing it on to the body chakras.

One of the key traits of a healthy fourth chakra is a loving sense of humor about the self. The healthy heart is dedicated to instinctual self-care, which relies on the physical, emotional, intellectual, and protective aspects of the three body chakras. However, the healthy heart helps to relieve the body chakra's intensities with humor.

The three body chakras exist in an atmosphere of danger and survival during much of their lives, and as such, don't often get the chance to relax. The healthy heart chakra is able to process some of their input in a less urgent, less survival-based light. The heart has somewhat more of an eagle-eye view, and can laugh at yet another intrusion, or more cords, or more physical and emotional ailments.

The laughter of the heart chakra is not derisive and self-immolating. It is a warm and knowing laughter that can help the body to gain a little distance and perspective in the face of trauma.

The heart can help to bring a little of the spirit's detachment into the body, but not so much that the body's reality is dismissed. Heart can rub a smashed shin and yell and laugh and channel healing energy into it while still being present with the pain. Heart laughter reduces stress in the body by giving it a small, healing break from the pain of the present moment.

Heart laughter also brings a healing awareness to the upper three chakras by reminding them that they are responsible for and connected to the body. Without the reality-based support of the fourth chakra, the three spirit chakras will go careening off into the blue and leave the body behind.

Sometimes, a crisis doesn't look like a crisis at all to the spirit, but like an excellent learning experience that will lead to ascendance. Without heart humor to bring it back to earth, humor that says, "Hello? I live on the planet in real time! I have to eat and sleep and pay the rent!" spirit would leap off cliff after cliff in search of enlightenment.

The healthy fourth chakra bestows humor, balance, self-love, acceptance of others, and a good connection between the spirit and body of its owner. The healthy fourth chakra also brings with it an empathy for the self that allows one to heal: to take time off, to create or choose loving environments, to seek out healing touch and healthy relationships, and to listen to the body.

The healthy heart heals others appropriately, as opposed to compulsively. It knows how to give without giving it all away.

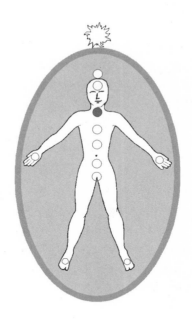

THE FIFTH CHAKRA

This clear sapphire blue, expressive chakra sits right above the hollow at the base of the neck, where it collects and examines communication from the spirit and the body, then sends it out into the world.

Because of its ability to channel the information of the spirit into real, tangible expression, the fifth chakra is also the center of change and commitment. The health of the fifth chakra relates not only to the level of communication possible at the present moment, but to the capacity for making and upholding change in the inner and outer self. In many cases, illnesses or blockages in the throat and neck, or headaches that originate in the neck, relate to an unwillingness to express oneself and commit to change.

The fifth chakra is also the center of the psychic ability of *clairaudience*, or the ability to hear disembodied voices and messages from the spirit world. Clairaudience is a difficult psychic ability to balance, especially since it is viewed in the Western medical model as a clear precursor of schizophrenia and other psychiatric disorders.

Since psychic abilities beyond intuition are unwelcome in the world of medicine, many unfortunate clairaudients are misdiagnosed as schizophrenic and routed into the world of drugs and institutionalization. Hearing voices is not given even the tiny credence that is lent to seeing visions. Clairaudients are usually offered no support, and no choice but to agree that they are insane and out of control. When placed on drugs that unground them and shoot them out of their bodies (which makes uncontrolled clairaudience more likely), true insanity usually follows.

Hard stuff, but it's all a part of life in a society that tries to live without spirituality. Life without spirit can't work, and unfortunately, the people who take the biggest hits are the people who have real but unprovable spiritual difficulties, for which there are no readily available answers.

Perhaps we, the spiritually educated, can use our fifth chakra ability to communicate the need for spiritual healing in psychiatric therapy. Perhaps we can change the dreadful legacy of zombiehood and lifelong institutionalization for humans in spiritual distress.

The frustration I have with the whole situation is that it's a fairly easy thing to heal a too-open, overly clairaudient fifth chakra. You just close it up a little with your hands, and cover the back and front of it with grounded Sentries as you renew your grounding and re-form your aura. Perhaps this information could be spread around a few mental hospitals and homeless shelters.

The fifth chakra can sometimes have very distinct energy and color discrepancies between its top and bottom halves. This is due to the often separate channelling duties it provides for the fourth chakra below it, and the sixth chakra above.

When the connection between the fourth and the fifth chakras is good, a person can express the needs of the body and the heart with clarity. In this instance, the energy in the lower half of the fifth chakra would be clear blue and moving well.

If the fourth-fifth connection is not good, the energy in the lower half of the fifth chakra will be dark, slow-moving, or deadened. In this case, you will very often find a person who gives too much, and cannot ask for help or nurturing, even though they want and need it. Men and women suffer this self-denying debility in about the same numbers, but women get more press for it.

When the connection between the fifth chakra and the clairvoyant sixth chakra is good, a person can share his intuitions, visions, and discerning abilities. In this instance, the energy in the top half of the fifth chakra will be clear blue and moving well. If the connection is bad, and clairvoyance is not acceptable in or outside of the self, the top half of the fifth chakra will be dark, slow moving, or strangely shaped.

The ability to communicate clairvoyant perceptions is generally more acceptable in men, who are often free to bring their clairvoyance into business if they just call it discernment or horse sense. Women's sixth chakra energy has been considered somewhat less valid and called intuition, which is now just another name for guessing. Because of a general lack of permission for women to be clairvoyant (though they can be empathic), females will oftentimes have completely darkened upper fifth and sixth chakras.

Often, a woman's ability (or a man's, if he runs a lot of feminine energy) to discern without emotion, which is a sixth chakra function, is invalidated and unused. Her empathic, emotive fourth chakra is often overused as a result, which unbalances her energy system as a whole and her fifth chakra in particular. She becomes a psychic unable to separate from her intuition, because the heart chakra's empathy hasn't got the balancing support of the sixth chakra's ability to separate, discern, and look at life from above. In this instance, her fifth chakra would not be very healthy, stuck as it is between two unwell and conflicting energy centers.

Men (or women who run a lot of masculine energy) will generally exhibit the opposite imbalance, in which the unemotional, discerning sixth chakra ability is over-utilized, while the emotive, loving qualities of the heart are under-utilized.

Men have lots of permission to know (from their clairvoyant sixth chakra), but very little permission to love, care, and connect (from their heart chakra). This societally-approved position creates men with very little empathy or human warmth, and probably a body/spirit split over time, as the fourth chakra energy becomes clogged through a lack of use. In this imbalance, the fifth chakra would also show signs of distress, overwork, and one-sidedness because it too is stuck between non-communicating fourth and sixth chakras.

Balance in both instances comes through healing the chakra system as a whole, and by being careful not to over-use (or ignore) any one chakra. As previously over-or-under-used chakras come back into balance and communication with one another, they will discover new and more holistic ways of functioning in the world. The old spirit/body or intellect/emotion splits become unnecessary.

I also see fifth chakra damage among people with strict religious backgrounds, where individual spiritual knowledge and discovery were frowned upon. In these cases, a controlling cord from the church or the parents is usually alive and active in the upper part of the fifth chakra.

This controlling cord seeks to stop any communication that is different from that of the religious group. It also helps to ensure an inability to change or commit to different belief styles. Please see the special cord-removal process at the end of this book if you suspect you have agreed to live your spiritual life with an iron-clad study guide.

A segmented, light-and-dark fifth chakra usually goes along with a general chakra system imbalance, especially in regard to an overburdened heart chakra. This burden can be due to the shutting off, *or* the over-use of the heart chakra.

When the damaged heart chakra is not available to channel physical-world information to the fifth chakra, or accept spiritual-world information from it, the fifth chakra will have to work in halves if it is going to work at all. In cases of heart-chakra overload, the fifth will still gather spirit information from the sixth and seventh chakras as it is supposed to do. Because it can't reliably off-load to the heart, however, it will just try to keep its upper half clean and working as best it can. In a sense, this fifth chakra will kill off a part of itself (the heart connection) so that the rest of it (the sixth-seventh chakra connection) can live.

What I see in such a case is a very spiritually attuned person whose "heart-love" healing or heart-closure creates an impossibly uncentered life. Because their fourth chakra is too busy to channel physical information to its own spirit chakras, I generally find a spirit/body split, and a lack of bodily self-awareness. I also find an unbalanced amount of spiritual information that makes the body's realities (such as emotions, financial issues, and human relationships) seem unreal and unimportant. Such people are often quite filled with spiritual information, but are unconnected to, and unable to live in, their bodies. They are often ill or very over-or-underweight due to a lack of grounding and safety in the body.

In cases of a very bright lower half of the fifth chakra (and a correspondingly darkened upper half), I see people whose psychic energy pretty much stops at empathy. For whatever reason, these people cannot hear or accept spiritual information. They feel everyone else's pain very deeply, but cannot separate from the world around them, or see a way out of distress.

Overly empathic people do not have the guiding, eagle-eyed support of the three spirit chakras, or the energy to commit themselves to change and growth. This may have been caused by a lack of permission to explore spirituality in their growing years, or it may have been self-created out of a fear of what would be seen or heard in the spiritual realm.

In many cases, an empath's spirit-body split occurs when they enter into a lifestyle that is at a cross-purpose to their true path. Detaching from and ignoring their spiritual information allows them to stay in wrong environments with the wrong people. Their overemphasis on heart information obscures the clairvoyant information of their sixth chakra. By segmenting their fifth chakra, they can more easily live or work in inappropriate environments without having to hear all the spiritual messages, chatter, and commandments that would get them back on their own path again.

I see this spirit/body and fifth chakra split very often in heart-chakra healers who live in abusive or imprisoning environments. Their sixth chakra spiritual knowledge, if channelled, would know exactly what was going on and would tell them in no uncertain terms to get the hell out. Also, their sixth chakra would probably get them in trouble by channelling itself down into the communicative fifth chakra, which would read the riot act, out loud, to their abusers.

I want to make a long story short, because we could go on forever about the causes of chakra deviations without ever healing them and getting on with life. If you have a bright half to your fifth chakra, it's a good thing, because it means that your fifth is alive and working to the best of its capabilities right now, even if you aren't.

Don't get married to the dark half of your fifth chakra. Just get your whole chakra system into balance, and clean up the connection between the dark half of your fifth and its neighboring chakra. If your fifth chakra has had the energy to keep half of itself working without your help, it won't have any trouble being whole when you get your act together. Be aware, though, because getting your act together from the fifth chakra's point of view could be jarring.

As I said, the fifth chakra is about change and commitment—these scare most people out of their minds. Both change and commitment require trust in the self and the universe. Trust is a major issue for those of us who were molested as children; however, that's not a sufficient excuse. Unmolested people have the same difficulties with fifth chakra energy as we do.

Change and commitment made from a fifth chakra perspective are serious, courageous, life-affirming adventures. If you have dreams of some life purpose very different from your present occupation, your healthy fifth chakra will pull you out of the mud or the clouds and help you sign up for classes, or quit your present job and move on. One small look around us will show that very few people in our society, molested or not, have healthy fifth chakras.

There is very little real support for the kind of self-affirming cliff-jumping the fifth chakra asks for. All sorts of books, movies, and television commercials exhort us to be brave and fearless. However, precious few friends and business associates would support us in, say, leaving nursing to be a nature photographer, or putting all our assets into a venture providing books to children in the Kalahari. We seem, as a society, to be somewhat able to support fictional or far-removed heroes, but unwilling to support change or the commitment to true ideals in ourselves or those around us.

My suggestion for supporting your fifth chakra is to seek out and befriend brave, active, and non-conforming people. You may find them in men's and women's groups, in church outreach programs, in the healing arts or local arts council, or out in nature pursuits. You will also find unwell people, egotists, and rabid runaway healers in these same places. Every now and then, however, you'll find a gem of a person in whom love and courage are stronger than fear and excuses. With people like this, you can begin to speak your truth and share your dreams and feelings. Then, your fifth chakra will begin to blossom.

Don't be surprised, though, if these brave people call you on any falseness they see. Fifth chakra people have almost no patience for whining and lies. They will not be able to support you in remaining in abusive, unhealthy environments or mind-sets, no matter how convincing your arguments may be. You'll need to hang out with the runaway fourth chakra healers if you want support in continuing to hurt yourself.

Because the healthy fifth chakra is all about communication, you will find its healing will require you to speak your truth. In general, only people with healthy fifth chakras will be able to hear your heartfelt truth. This is why it is so important to find them as you commit to yourself and your changes. Without the human support of other fifth chakra people, this aspect of your spiritual journey could be an utter fiasco, especially if your life is filled with powerless, excuse-filled, and emotionally controlling people.

To the fearful and stuck, fifth chakra energy is unwelcome. It reminds others that, yes, they could change and get out of their rut if they would only commit to themselves. However, such commitment means ending blame and excuses, and accepting total responsibility for their destiny. This is terrifying.

Being a victim of other people and of blind chance and circumstance is a very empowering thing, because it takes all personal responsibility away. Inside the world of victimhood, people are powerless, which means they have no responsibility. Bad guys and bad energy control them, and there is nothing to do but give up. It's actually comfortable to feel this way, because it means that no action is necessary. Life is simply bad, nobody gets out alive, and if it isn't one thing, it's another.

Well, the fifth chakra doesn't take this view. It sees abusive people and environments and either tries to change them, or leaves them far behind. It won't waste its precious days and hours in places where no growth occurs. It sees "negativity" as a challenge, not a life sentence. It speaks its mind when lies are present (which can make for very uncomfortable social gatherings), and it commits itself to change and growth, which can frighten conservative people. In essence, the commitment of fifth chakra energy is very unsettling to anyone not doing their work.

Your work with your healthy fifth chakra will shake up the psychic fabric around you. If you've forgotten the whole stasis thing from *Rebuilding the Garden*, you might be astonished at the blockages your friends and family may put in your way. They may try to terrify you out of making change and movement. They may question and degrade everything you say, and everything you commit to. Or, you may attempt to do this to yourself in response to cords that flourish in your fifth chakra.

The solution? Use your skills to center and ground yourself, destroy images, burn contracts, and separate from the old mind-sets. Your healthy and functioning fifth chakra will help you do all this by adding the energy of commitment and dedication to your cleansing and separation work.

When you work with fifth chakra energy, you may experience throat and neck problems that arise in response to old fears and contracts. When your body signals blockages in your fifth chakra, it is very healing to place your fingers gently on your throat and say out loud, as writer and healer Louise Hay does, "I'm willing to change, I'm willing to change, I'm willing to change." This can become a wry, laughter-filled action when you notice which relationships, ideas, or movements make you clear your throat, cough, or suddenly throw your neck out. Some concepts may even make you feel as if you are going to cough up a fur-ball. These are the ones that require contract burning. You're willing to change, you're willing to change....

OPEN OR CLOSED FIFTH CHAKRA

A wide-open fifth chakra in an unhealthy chakra system needs to be healed immediately. Because the fifth chakra is a very unused chakra in our present-day world, it seems to attract much unusual energy and attention. The possibility exists for unbalanced others to cord into your too-open fifth chakra, which can cause hearing problems, clairaudience, throat and neck pain, and an inability to communicate effectively.

These are all the effects of living in a society in turmoil over change, communication, and commitment to higher ideals; however, we can separate our fifth chakras from the unwell society around us and live our own lives unmolested by toxic beliefs. The fifth chakra in this instance should be sized back down to its healthy three-to-five inch diameter, and covered, front and back, with grounded Sentries.

A temporarily open fifth chakra in a healthy chakra system (with a well-functioning heart chakra, and a very clear sixth chakra) is a sign that one is opening to new levels of commitment, communication, and awareness. This opening may be accompanied by neck vertebra dislocations, or a cleansing, coughing, mucous-filled cold.

In this case, please place grounded Sentries at the front and the back of your open fifth chakra, and see your acupuncturist, chiropractor, or massage therapist for support in clearing blockages from your body. Your fifth chakra should size itself back to normal within a week or so. If not, please perform a full chakra reading to ascertain whether you should re-size your fifth chakra, or let it remain open for a few more days. Because it is the center of communication, your fifth chakra will have no problem telling you how it wants to look and what it needs you to do.

A closed fifth chakra in an unhealthy or unbalanced chakra system is a sign of unwillingness to grow, change, listen, communicate, or be connected to spirit. This closing can be done out of fear (especially the fear of clairaudience), or with a "No one can tell me what to do!" temper tantrum energy.

Oh my goodness. There's nothing as stubborn as a person with a stubbornly closed fifth chakra. They commit themselves to doing nothing with an intensity that almost makes them feel as if they are doing their work! They usually have chronic neck or throat blockages that accessorize their chronic life blockages nicely.

Closed fifth chakra people are, by far, the hardest people to work with. They will go a certain distance in their growth, and then trash themselves and anyone who tries to help them when things get hard. Like the fifth chakra energy they try so hard to squelch, they are focused, communicative, and committed, but unfortunately, only when it comes to protecting their position. For a person with a blocked-up, closed-off fifth chakra, that position is usually illness, obstruction, and justification.

An example: I have seen suicidal people with blockages of all kinds, most of which can be released through emotional channelling. However, I can spot a closed fifth suicidal rage by one determining factor: the person will fight like crazy for their pain. They will actually yell and stomp off if anyone suggests that they could feel other feelings, or live life another way. They will defend their suicidal urges as a lioness would protect her cub. People with closed fifth chakras are unbelievably defended.

This stubborn, temper tantrum energy usually brings forward the fifth chakra energy of others. Confrontations ensue. Because any fifth chakra can get right to the meaty center of any issue, things can get pretty pointed and uncomfortable. Fifth chakra fights can be very ugly in their absolute, unblinking truth, but sometimes, such fights are necessary to clear out all the crap that builds up around a closed fifth chakra.

If your fifth chakra is closed, you can break up the blockages yourself by sitting down and listening to yourself. Your usual state of confusion and stasis comes from closing off your ability to hear.

In the healthy chakra model, confusion comes up only rarely. Healthy fifth chakra energy channels spiritual truth, physical knowledge, and the commitment to balance and nurture the self. When you are closed off, and cannot use these fifth chakra attributes, confusion reigns. The way to end the confusion, besides having someone yell at you, is to sit and listen to yourself as you heal your chakras.

The constant turmoil in your life is not natural, nor is it par for the course. It is unnatural, and unnecessary. Pain, drama, and turmoil are a part of life, but not the be-all and end-all of existence. You can lighten up and let your defenses and justifications go. You can live as you wish to live, and you can connect to your dreams and hopes.

You can move on from limiting environments, and you can change your health picture, or at least your outlook about your health. You can dream of accomplishments and plan to change your career, and you can imagine a healing love life. You can create meaning that is specific to you, even if the world around you is meaningless. Your open fifth chakra will help you do all of this and more. These are not silly ideals.

It is a good idea to hang out with the fifth chakra people I wrote about a few pages back if you want support in renewing your ability to hear, speak, change, and commit to your life. These people are truly alive. They see the ugliness of life, but they don't let it stop them from creating their own meaning. They say, "Sure, life sucks, everyone blames everyone else, evil is real, and mosquitoes won't go away, but I have this really good idea for solar cars, or a wish to travel and teach, or a need to play music, so I'm going to be happy in spite of it all."

People with healthy, open fifth chakras aren't happy idiots who live in a dream world. They are active, aware, and caring members of society who have fun because they live their dreams every day.

Once again I am going to tell you this: you may feel free to have issues with communication, commitment, and change, but don't hurt your fifth chakra in the process. If you close it down, you will find yourself incredibly stuck in a very short, yet excruciating period of time. Go ahead and be as stubborn as you like, but let your fifth chakra live its life unmolested by you or anyone else, please!

The fifth can close itself off and take a vacation when the other chakras are healthy enough to let it do so. If your other chakras are up and working, and your neck, throat, and ears are clear even though your fifth chakra is closed, congratulations!

You can support your fifth chakra's vacation by placing a congratulatory hello gift in front of each of your open chakras, and by placing a protective Sentry in front and in back of your closed fifth. Your vacationing fifth chakra should come back on line in a week or so. If not, ask it what would need to happen for it to open back up. Usually, your fifth chakra will require a new aura and grounding system to keep it safe from cording. It will also require your commitment to listen to and act upon its information. Good luck.

TRAITS OF A HEALTHY FIFTH CHAKRA: People with healthy fifth chakras often say the strangest things, or hear the strangest truths in mundane conversations. Their communicative skills are highly attuned, and even if they do not consider themselves psychic, they usually are.

Fifth chakra people have a very active awareness that makes them good communicative healers, speakers, or therapists. They are also very reliable, because when they make a commitment, they follow through. However, unlike a heart chakra person who may commit beyond fatigue and sanity, the fifth chakra person will commit only to those things that resonate deeply for them.

Fifth chakra people may be hard to keep up with. They may even look flaky to some. They commit to things wholeheartedly, then leave when their commitments do not provide service, healing, or meaning. They do not leave people in the lurch, but they do follow the dictates of their own internal knowledge, which is unlike anyone else's.

Being in the life of a fifth chakra person can be exhausting if you try to keep up with them, but keeping up is not the point. If you tried to commit to their commitments, or believe in their beliefs, you'd be off your own path in a matter of hours. The best way to live with a fifth chakra person is to get your own fifth chakra in shape, and to find your own dreams, meaning, and beliefs with their loving (if unorthodox) support and example.

As I said before, fifth chakra people are very insightful and supportive if you want to hear the truth, and very annoying and rude if you don't. In living with or relating to them, you must be willing to hear the truth, to speak the truth, and to live your truth. Otherwise, it's going to be a bumpy, lonely ride. If you have a fifth chakra person in your life, stop resisting and bless them. They, more than anyone else (besides you and your guides), will keep you honest and on path. Let them. They need your friendship and your love.

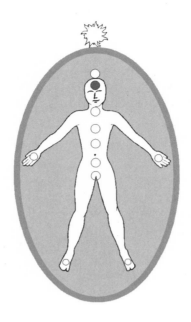

FURTHER INTO THE GARDEN

THE SIXTH CHAKRA
(OR THIRD EYE)

This brilliant indigo-colored, receptive chakra sits right in the center of the forehead, between the eyebrows and the hairline. The sixth chakra is the center of *clairvoyance*, or the ability to receive energy vibrations visually. When people try to contact us or cord into us psychically, the clairvoyant sixth chakra is often the first chakra alerted. It is usually a very active, very busy, and very communicative chakra.

The sixth chakra is also the center of the more earthly skills of discernment and sound, unemotional judgment, as well as the center of higher brain functions of learning and information processing and retrieval. Sixth chakra energy confers a focused consciousness that blends nicely with the grounded, emotive, protective, empathic, and communicative chakra energies below it.

With the support of a healthy sixth chakra, one has a level of certainty about self, path, and the needs of others. This certainty can seem cold and detached to less aware people, or to people too heavily dependent on heart chakra attributes. Sixth chakra energy sees things as they are—not as they pretend to be, not as they should be—but as they are.

The healthy, aware sixth chakra helps its owner make decisions based on facts instead of hope. The sixth chakra's unemotional certainty, coupled with the decisive, committed communication and action of the healthy fifth chakra, can be unsettling to people who prefer excuses over action.

When the heart chakra looks at the pain of others or the self, it moves to empathy, care, love, and healing from a close, personal standpoint. The heart understands and empathizes with pain, and has limitless emotional patience. The sixth chakra looks at the pain of others or the self from a different viewpoint.

The sixth chakra sees not just the pain, but the issues behind the pain. It sees the level of comfort the pain provides, the amount of time the pain has been allowed to be present, and how the pain generates the empathy and attention of family and friends. The sixth chakra sees how much work has been done to process the pain, and the willingness to release the pain and move on to something else. The sixth chakra regularly asks questions that the emotive fouth chakra would consider jarring, non-supportive, or unloving.

In this time of victim-consciousness and inner child work, which is all from third and fourth chakra awareness, the emotionless, truth-seeking mission of the sixth chakra is not supported, courted, or appreciated. Sixth chakra energy can be annoying and even threatening to people who need to maintain their victim status in response to their childhood traumas, or in the face of their less-than-healthy adult choices. Sixth chakra energy has very little patience for victim consciousness.

In response, most people shut off their own sixth chakras so they don't have to know the truth, about themselves and their true responsibilities, or about the people they allow into their lives. Shutting off obscures information about true life path and purpose too—people with closed sixth chakras don't have to think about their work and relationship responsibilities. This can make for a nice vacation, because closing off the questing, truth-at-all-costs sixth chakra can provide a little bit of peace and quiet.

The problem with closing off is that the sixth chakra also holds the ability to discern properly in everyday situations, and to process and qualify the information coming into the brain. Therefore, people whose sixth chakras have been closed for a period of months or years tend not to have a clue, not just about the big spiritual questions, but about mundane things as well.

People with closed sixth chakras choose strange relationships, and go-nowhere jobs. They don't know what they want to do, or how they feel about things. They move from place to place, and from idea to idea, with no logical thread. They don't have tangible dreams of purpose, or even of a better life. Such people often have a number of brain dysfunctions that go along with their dysfunctional lives.

People with closed sixth chakras may be forgetful and undependable. They may have difficulties processing information, trouble reading or writing, and may experience sudden thought-or-word loss and periodic stuttering. All of these dysfunctions usually diminish when the sixth chakra is up and running again.

Re-opening the sixth chakra requires personal bravery. When the sixth chakra has been closed for a period of time, one tends to career off-path. When the sixth re-opens, it asks the hard questions immediately: "What are we doing here? Why does our body look and feel like this? What happened to our art and our dreams? Who are all these strange people, and what the hell is going on here?" If you have no excuses, explanations, or answers, congratulate yourself. It means you're on your way home.

The beautiful thing (or the horrible thing, depending on your attitude) about sixth chakra questions is that they require no answer. All you can really do is accept the information (or the rebuke), and move from acceptance to processing and action.

Sixth chakra questions and remarks often leave people dumbfounded and speechless. The sixth might look at a searing pain in someone's arm or low back and ask, "When did you first want to strangle your mother?" or, "How many people rely on you to do all their emotional work for them?"

Though the information from the sixth chakra is often startling, it provides a strange comfort in its own way. The sixth chakra sees through all the garbage. If you like your garbage more than your health, you won't want sixth chakra energy in yourself or anyone around you. If you are committed to your health and happiness, no matter what, sixth chakra energy will be your new best friend.

OPEN OR CLOSED SIXTH CHAKRA

A wide open (anything larger than five inches in diameter) sixth chakra in an unbalanced chakra system can cause a myriad of problems, from an onslaught of psychic visions and vivid dreams, to a brain full of racing and contradictory thoughts.

Wide-open sixth chakras can also bring so much energy into the brain that its synapses will fire in response, creating tics, shooting pains, migraines, and seizures. The eyes can become blurry, tired, or hyper-sensitive to allergens when too much uncontrolled energy is present in the sixth chakra. A wide-open sixth can also make the room in the head jangly and uninhabitable.

Usually, the sixth chakra will open too wide when the other chakras are off-kilter. When the second chakra is uncentered and sponging energy from others, the sixth will often open to try and provide discernment to the essentially non-discerning second chakra. Sponging is so ungrounding, though, that the sixth chakra will soon be off-kilter as well.

When the third chakra is not protecting the aura and the body, the sixth will open wide and try to work as a psychic first-defense system. The sixth will clairvoyantly decide who is safe and who is not. Without having the third chakra available to protect it, the sixth will often get smacked and corded by people who would rather not be looked at quite so closely.

When the fourth chakra is pouring all the heart energy out of the body in runaway healing, the sixth chakra will often open wide to provide the same discernment it offers to a sponge-happy second. Since the heart in this instance is unavailable to connect body and spirit, the entire system soon becomes unstable and ungrounded. Also, the unhealthy heart will often fight with the sixth for dominance ("My energy is better than yours!"), which squashes the poor fifth chakra between two warring nations.

I want to remind you that your chakras are symbols of your awareness. Your awareness directs their actions. If you've got a war between your fourth and sixth chakras, you have personally created a conflict between your empathic abilities and your discerning abilities. Your chakras are only illuminating this conflict for you.

Your chakras are not acting as free agents. When they are unbalanced, they are following your lead. You can heal them and regain control of all your previously warring aspects. When you do, your healthy chakra system will support you, as much as it can, in maintaining your new balance.

Please close an unbalanced and open sixth chakra as soon as you can, and perform a complete chakra system healing. With an unhealthy open sixth, you can expect to see imbalances throughout your system. Thank your sixth chakra for trying to keep you safe in spite of yourself.

Also, remember that your sixth chakra is often a first-contact chakra for psychic communication. People will very often try to tune into or cord into your sixth chakra in order to get to know you, or to get information from you.

If your sixth chakra is wide open, unprotected, and existing in an unbalanced chakra system, these psychic contacts can be very disconcerting. You may have frontal-lobe headaches, visions, trouble concentrating or thinking, and trouble sleeping, because so much foreign energy is inside your sixth chakra. Please cover your sixth chakra, even after you perform a complete chakra system healing, with at least six or seven grounded Sentries, front and back. This will help your sixth chakra to remain healthy when cording people come knocking again.

The special Gift Facial taught in the *Rebuilding the Garden* is very helpful in pulling energy off the face, the eyes, and out of the sixth chakra. Try it.

In a healthy, grounded chakra system, the sixth chakra will open to accept new information about life path and clairvoyant abilities. The sixth will also open to allow a spiritual healing of brain and vision dysfunctions.

My suggestion is that a healthy, wide-open sixth chakra be watched carefully from the room in the head. Even in a robust system, a wide-open sixth chakra can attract too much attention from the psychic fabric around you. The healthy opening of the sixth chakra is an exciting evolutionary process—your friends and family may want to share this process with you. Though they probably mean well, their attention, focus, and possible cording can affect you, spiritually and physically.

Because the sixth chakra is directly inside the brain, its energy-attracting openness can affect not only your clairvoyant abilities, but your thought-processing abilities as well. Therefore, I would allow it to stay wide open for two to three days at the very most, unless you have a hermitage available.

If you do not have a place where you can have long stretches of peace and solitude, please re-size your sixth chakra within three days. Use your hands to return it to its normal three-to-five-inch diameter, or envision it closing as a camera shutter does.

If you have a peaceful, solitary place to stay, go there and let your sixth stay open for a week or so. It will be safer to be a totally open and receptive clairvoyant if you are alone.

In either case, place a protective Sentry in front of each of your chakras, and at least six grounded Sentries directly in front and in back of your sixth chakra until you get it back to size.

A closed sixth chakra in an unbalanced chakra system is a sign of closing off the clairvoyant ability, and the more usual discerning, processing intelligence. As you can imagine, this makes a conscious life nearly impossible; however, it does make an unconsciously suicidal, off-path life more bearable. For a while.

It takes a great deal of energy to keep a sixth chakra closed—it's like trying to keep the eyes closed when there are dangers in the environment. The body will pop the eyes open to get its bearings, whether you want to see or not. It is the same with the sixth chakra. The sixth chakra is the eye of the spirit. It is the part of us that receives pictures of the energetic world around us. Closing the sixth chakra requires a constant and nearly exhausting struggle to stay asleep.

I have seen many people attempt to keep their sixth chakras shut, but such self-imposed blindness never leads anywhere. Closed sixth chakra people are often so far off path that they don't even think a path exists for them. They tend to scoff at paths in general. They are the eternal unmagical naysayers, squashing the dreams of anyone who attempts to awaken in their presence. My own sixth chakra can't stand people like this. It has been hurt terribly by the sleeping people.

This is my sixth chakra talking now: Wake up! Any path that is not your own is dangerous to you. Any relationship, job, choice, or idea that does not feed you eats off of you. Happiness can only come when you are truly and unashamedly yourself. You must look; you must watch; you must see; you must feel. You must live your life as yourself and stop making excuses, or you will live and die in pain that has no meaning.

Ouch! My empathic fourth chakra is going crazy over that one! Oh my gosh, it's doing back flips to make room and give permission for all the off-path and de-selfed positions we have to take every day. But my sixth chakra sticks by its information.

This is an interesting illumination of the kind of communication that goes on in a connected chakra system. As each chakra wakes up, its information is added to the whole. Sometimes the information makes sense to the other chakras, sometimes it doesn't. Our job is to strive for balance in the midst of what may seem to be conflicting information.

In truth, the fourth and the sixth chakras are doing the same work. The fourth chakra is not less-evolved or stupid. It knows that the unflinching information of the sixth is true, but from the almost-body, almost-spirit position it inhabits, the fourth chakra can see physical reality, which is not as cut-and-dried as spiritual reality.

The fourth chakra sees the pain humans go through in trying to become whole, and it has empathy for that struggle. The fourth sees where humans are heading, which is toward spiritual certainty, but it also knows the difficult reality of life on this planet; therefore, it has more patience than the spirit-centered sixth chakra.

When the fourth and sixth chakras can communicate freely (through a healthy, unsegmented fifth chakra), the fourth will spend less time making excuses for off-path behavior, while the sixth will lighten up and offer guidance in a gentler way. This balance can only be achieved if the sixth is allowed to open up and live again.

At first, the communication from a previously shut-off sixth chakra will be somewhat strident. With frequent healings and work with the grounding cord, the aura, and the separation tools, the sixth chakra will attain a place of balance within the whole.

Here is the sixth chakra message above from a more balanced perspective: Any path that is not your own can be dangerous if you forget who you are, but all paths have meaning if you remain awake and aware. Any relationship, job, choice, or idea that does not feed you eats off of you, and sometimes, what is eaten lightens your load and frees you for the next step in your journey. Happiness can only come when you are truly and unashamedly yourself. This takes time, support, study, trust, and love. You must live your life as yourself and stop making excuses, for yourself or anyone else, or you will die without ever living.

Opening your sixth chakra after a period of darkness may require you to take a few days off from your life and responsibilities. Successfully opening your sixth chakra may also require you to change your life and amend your responsibilities.

Once again, the support of healthy fifth/sixth chakra people will be needed, because this is not a fun process to do all by yourself. You will require people around you who honor dreams, individuality, and spiritual purpose. If you cannot find such people in your life, please visit a book store or a library and let your sixth chakra choose some supportive and empowering books on healing, career changes, conscious relationships, religious or spiritual teachings, and love in general. Don't pick up too many victim-consciousness books, though. Your sixth will become grumpy if you try to wallow in past issues right now.

The sixth chakra likes to look inside and ahead of you, at your heart, your dreams, and your connection to God. It does not like to spend its time outside and behind you with perpetrators, past injuries, and old stories. The old stories make it too easy to go back to sleep. Open your sixth chakra and point it at yourself—let it help to lead you back home.

The healthy sixth can close off and take a vacation when the chakra system as a whole is in balance. A closed sixth chakra in a healthy system also signals a fairly healthy exterior life. Because the sixth is so vigilant and responsible (bossy, even), it will not usually close off if there is the possibility of danger in your environment. If you find a closed sixth in your healthy chakra system, congratulate not only your other chakras, but yourself as well. You've placed yourself in a supportive, conscious, and healing environment for the most part. You've been doing your work!

You can tell that your sixth chakra is taking a healthy vacation by the condition of your other chakras—specifically by the health of the upper portion of your fifth chakra, which should be bright blue and moving well. You will also be free of headaches, eyestrain, and confusion, and you will be able to stay in the room in your head, even though your sixth chakra is closed for now.

Your sixth chakra will close when it needs to review its information, re-connect with the pure spiritual information of the seventh chakra, or remove cords and old clairvoyant relating patterns that unground the body.

While your sixth chakra is healing itself, please give each of your other chakras and yourself a congratulatory hello gift. Cover your aura with a blanket of strongly grounded Sentries. Place a grounded Sentry in front and in back of your sixth chakra, and let it stay closed for up to a week if it wants to.

Because it is so vigilant and responsible, your sixth chakra will not usually stay closed for more than a few days. If your life is safe enough, though, it may be able to stay closed for a little longer.

To support your vacationing sixth chakra, stay in the room in your head and keep an eye on your sixth chakra until the week is up. If your sixth chakra has not re-opened by the end of the seventh day, ask it what it needs from you. It may require a material change in your life, the release of certain relationships, a dedication to specific goals, or a strengthening of your separation skills.

Be prepared. When your sixth chakra re-opens for business, your life will be excitingly different.

TRAITS OF A HEALTHY SIXTH CHAKRA: People with active sixth chakras have access to amazing amounts of information. If their sixth chakra is active in response to the inactivity of their other chakras, the information will often be about other people and other events. If their sixth chakra is a part of a healthy, active, and balanced chakra system, the information will refer more specifically to themselves, their health and wellness, and their own life path.

This is an important distinction. Many gifted psychics have extremely active sixth chakras that allow them to access information about and for their clients. These same psychics, however, often need tremendous support in order to keep their own lives on track. Like runaway fourth-chakra healers who cannot make time for themselves, runaway sixth-chakra clairvoyants cannot find truth for themselves. All their clairvoyant energy is used on and for others. In a healthy chakra system where sixth chakra energy is honored, protected, and used primarily on and for the self, the individual tends to stay on track and on path without too much effort.

When people have a healthy and balanced sixth chakra, they are naturally clairvoyant, which means that their clairvoyance is not flamboyant and dramatic. Instead of seeing lotto numbers and plane crashes in the Andes, they find antique wedding dresses for their friends in thrift stores. They find vital information about their child's health or their life's path through visiting a strange bookstore in a strange town because they thought they should. Healthy clairvoyance is just as magical and inexplicable as the more lurid or thrilling clairvoyance of famous psychics, but because it has more to do with quiet, inner reality, it gets less press.

A healthy self-clairvoyant does not have a lot of unanswered questions, or a deep need for money, fame, and security. The very act of being on path, whatever that path is, creates support and comfort for healthy clairvoyants, even if it doesn't look that way from the outside. Their life paths may take them into unfamiliar areas, into poverty, into conflicts, or away from everything familiar, but still they feel secure.

The life path of healthy sixth chakra people is clear, though it may be difficult. They are able to find support for their path in unusual or "magical" ways that seem perfectly normal to them. They are able to process input, lessons, and information with ease and speed, and they are very often treasured counselors among people who want to live spiritually attuned lives.

Sixth chakra people are often removed from the people around them, just as sixth chakra energy is removed from our everyday world. If the fact of their uniqueness does not separate them, their blinding truthfulness usually will. They can find true comradeship with other healthy sixth-chakra people, but with unbalanced or less attuned people, they will always appear to be separate ... treasured, maybe, but separate nevertheless.

If you are fortunate enough to have a balanced sixth chakra person in your life, you will have an honest friend, and support in making your transition to sixth chakra awareness. Love them, include them in your life, and soon you will see that they are not strange or otherworldly. They are just doing their work. So can you.

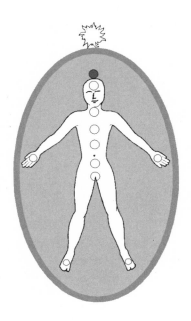

FURTHER INTO THE GARDEN

THE SEVENTH
(OR CROWN) CHAKRA

This violet-colored, receptive chakra sits above the very top of the head. It almost floats over the body. It is the first out-of-body chakra. The seventh chakra is the center of our bodily connection to pure spiritual energy and information, whether that be our own higher spiritual energy, the energy and information of our spirit guides and angels, the energy of other, unrelated beings without bodies, or the energy and information of God.

The seventh chakra contains the blueprint (or violetprint, in this case) of spiritual purpose we agreed upon before we entered our bodies and our usually confusing and unspiritual lives. Because so much of our time is spent in confusion between spirit and body, pure seventh chakra energy is often ignored, shut off, corded, squashed, or damaged.

If you think it's hard to live from the pure commitment of the fifth chakra, or the pure knowledge of the sixth chakra in this world of trivia and violence, you ain't seen nothing yet. The seventh chakra contains absolute certainty and absolute purpose. It is pure spirit. And living from the seventh chakra on this planet can be pure hell.

The seventh chakra, because it is not centered inside the body, has very little connection to the mundane aspects of real life. Though its information on direction, purpose, spiritual journeys, soul mates, and right livelihood is vital, the seventh chakra speaks from a place little understood by ninety-five percent of the humans on this planet.

It is as if the seventh chakra speaks a dead language that only scholars can interpret. In an unbalanced chakra system, it doesn't even speak of the time-space continuum. Its spiritual information, though often valid, will have no real application to a human who needs to know *when* to make a move, *how* to get there, *where* to get the money, and *who* to contact.

In a very balanced and aware chakra system, the information from the seventh can be filtered and communicated to the body through the intellectual sixth, the communicative fifth, and the empathic heart. Even then, its information is often strange and otherworldly.

When the chakras are balanced and active, and the energy body is grounded, cleaned out, and centered inside a protected aura, the information from the seventh chakra provides clear (but not always comforting) direction.

When the energy is balanced after a long, confused, abuse-filled fallow period, the information from the seventh chakra can be terrifying. It knows with certainty that much work must be done to get back to the correct path. This path very often seems out-of-reach to people who have been living in abuse and despair.

In essence, you may find yourself married with four children and an abusive spouse and living in the Mid-west, when your seventh chakra points out that your true destiny lies in Cambodia, or in an alternative doctoral program. It's easy to see why seventh chakra information is generally ignored on this planet. It's just not practical.

Here's a message from my seventh: Not *practical*? Is it practical to incarnate with a specific life purpose, only to forget it as soon as puberty hits? Is it practical to stay on the earth plane for ten to twenty lifetimes because you keep forgetting why you went to the earth in the first place? Is it practical to scrabble around like a little pack rat, gathering this pointless item or that pointless experience, instead of living to the limit of your being and your essence?

Each of you has purpose and meaning. Each of you has the ability to heal yourself and your specific portion of the earth experience, but no one seems to care. I ask you to study homeopathy or Chinese medicine and heal the world, and I get money excuses, time excuses, logistical excuses and whining, while people who don't need to suffer do so by the thousands.

I ask you to create art and music, but I get talent excuses, fear excuses, and permission excuses while children's minds and hearts lie fallow, and the majesty of art is used for vodka ads. I exhort you to reach out to people, but I get ridiculous excuses while people on this planet die alone of "unacceptable" diseases, or live out their psychiatric distress, or retardation, or old age, locked up in places that no sane or practical person would call a home.

I am not impractical. The people on this planet are impractical, and they become more so every moment, precisely because my information is ignored. For every problem on this planet, spirit has placed ten thousand living people who are able to help—ten thousand specific people who have a specific, practical part in healing the difficulties of the earth, and in helping the humans, animals, plants, and mineral beings who live here.

Do even ten percent of these ten thousand people help, or do they surround themselves with ten thousand excuses about how hard everything is? Do they even recycle their *garbage*, for Spirit's sake? No. They just recycle their excuses, and tell me spirituality is impractical while the beautiful earth struggles under the killing weight of all their practicality.

End of sermon.

OPEN OR CLOSED SEVENTH CHAKRA

A very open (anything larger than five inches in diameter) seventh chakra in an unbalanced chakra system is often a sign of a spirit gasping for air in a very unspiritual life. When the seventh chakra is wide open, its owner is often seeking tremendous support from the spiritual plane in order to survive an ungrounded, unprotected daily life. In these cases, the body/spirit skew is often extreme.

The first order of business when the seventh chakra is wide open and overburdened is to create a room in the head that is grounded and securely anchored. In cases of seventh chakra malfunction, I often see floating rooms, rooms with no walls or ceiling, or hazy and indistinct rooms that cannot be used. These must be dealt with immediately.

Though grounding the body is just as important as keeping a usable room in the head, a very open seventh chakra tends to keep people out of their bodies completely. This makes grounding impossible. Getting the attention into the head is an easier first step in these instances, because it centers awareness fairly close to the seventh chakra. When the room in the head can be used and grounded, the spirit tends to settle itself back into the body so that first-or-feet chakra grounding is possible.

Closing up a wide-open seventh chakra requires one to open up the rest of the chakras, specifically the body-centered lower three. Starting over at the beginning of *Rebuilding the Garden* may be called for, as well as performing a complete chakra reading/healing. A wide-open seventh chakra needs complete attention, because it can create difficulties with grounding and living in the body.

A wide-open seventh in an unbalanced chakra system is as serious a call for help as a *kundalini* rush from an unbalanced first chakra. The wide-open first chakra is a defense system for the body—it ensures survival in the face of danger. The wide-open seventh chakra is a defense system for the spirit—it ensures survival in the face of an un-spiritual life. Heal this chakra and get back to the work of living your life, please.

The seventh chakra will open in a healthy and balanced chakra system—especially one where the heart fosters an excellent connection between body and spirit—in order to renew and rededicate its connection to the spiritual realm and God.

In some cases, the seventh chakra will open to collect new orders when life purpose has been achieved and it is not yet time for the body to die. Or, it will open when life-and-lesson contracts have been burnt sufficiently to allow new information and new direction to flow down from spirit. When the seventh chakra opens, it always signals exciting new direction, information, and purpose. Get ready!

When your seventh chakra is open, remember to protect it and all your other chakras with grounded Sentries, front and back. Please close it by the end of a week, unless it specifically asks to stay open for a longer period of time. If your chakra system is balanced, your seventh chakra will know what physical time means, and it will be able to tell you when it will close back down to its normal size. Protect it while it's open, and use this time to get your daily life in order. You may soon have new travel plans.

A tightly closed or very small (anything smaller than three inches in diameter) seventh chakra in an unbalanced chakra system is a sign of a refusal to listen to spirit, to believe in the spiritual world, or to communicate with God.

Closed and damaged seventh chakras are very common these days, especially among intellectuals, fanatically religious people, and cult members. In the latter two cases, seventh chakra damage comes from without, from an often punishing or closed-minded experience of God, and the damage usually involves controlling cords from the church or cult, or its leaders.

In the case of intellectuals, the damage to the seventh chakra comes from within, from an unwillingness to fall into "blind" or anti-intellectual faith. Intellectual groups such as academic or atheistic societies can also unconsciously cord into the seventh chakras of their members to make sure that nothing but the prescribed and agreed-upon information gets through. Please see the special chapter on cording at the end of this book for more specific information on this chakra-damaging communication technique.

When the seventh chakra is closed, life becomes a temporal experience: an experience of the five senses only. Even the intuitive skills of the other chakras become commonplace. The sixth chakra's clairvoyance becomes "horse sense," discernment, and plain old lucky guessing. The fifth chakra's clairaudience becomes "a little birdie," and so on.

Everything becomes commonplace, easily explainable, and achingly dull. Wonderful experiences of spiritual synchronicity are seen as coincidences, or examples of random chance. Healing pilgrimages to Lourdes are seen as prime examples of mass hysteria, and every bit of magic or divine talent is brought down to the mundane level of human understanding, or the understanding agreed upon by one's church or group.

Opening your seventh chakra in the face of group pressure or intellectual stubbornness requires courage, but it also requires a certain silliness. In the early stages of opening, it may require you to see every common thing as magical, whereas before, every magical thing was seen as commonplace.

When you walk, you can see the movement of your body as magical (how does your foot know to move itself?). When you eat, you can see the transfer from matter to energy as magical (how do your cells know to break your dinner into nutrients?). Your television, car, and computer are absolute wonders undreamed of just one hundred years ago, and powerful emperors of the not-so-distant past would have given everything just to have your clean running water and the use of your toilet on special ceremonial occasions! Think about it!

This world, every second of every day, is magical, and spiritual, and inexplicably complex. We think religion and intellect can bring the whole planet into some sort of rational order, but they can't. If you've ever met a true holy person, or a real genius, you know that they are absolutely filled with childlike wonder and millions of unanswerable questions. They don't know everything—they don't even pretend to!

Top-level scientists and religious leaders can explain a heck of a lot, but they know that they can't possibly explain it all. They're too busy exploring, testing, asking, experiencing, and living to presume to know the whole story of the universe, or the whole mind of God. Those with vast intellect and deep spirituality are not separate from magic and wonders.

If your seventh chakra is closed off for any reason, you may long for rationality, or some God-like control of all the answers, but closing off won't bring that. Deep understanding requires meaning, connection, and purpose, or the facts, figures, and information gathered rationally will never gel into anything deep or useful.

Even fourth-rate scientists know that without a working theory or overview, experimentation and fact-finding are useless. When you close (or allow anyone or any group to close) your seventh chakra, you sever your access to the meaning, connection, and over-viewing purpose of your spirit.

Any fact-finding endeavor undertaken with a closed seventh chakra, especially one that attempts to explain the meaning of life or God, will have no meaning because it will have no constructive overview. Each of us can only find the meaning of life, and the love of God, through the channel set up specifically for that purpose. That channel is our own working seventh chakra.

I am not in any way saying that religions and intellectual pursuits are wrong, or even damaging. Right now, we are talking specifically about an injured chakra. When the seventh chakra is open and healthy, religious study and group pursuits have their healing place. There is nothing intrinsically wrong with group experience unless the group requires seventh chakra damage in order to remain a cohesive unit. If group communication or any relationship requires chakras and auras and personalities to be damaged and truncated, they're bad. If not, they're good. You can figure out the rest for yourself.

Though your seventh chakra's spiritual path and information may not look good at a dinner party or church social, and may not be scientifically provable, it will be completely rational for you. Only your own spiritual information will work in your life. Sometimes, though, the teachings of Jesus or Buddha or Bokonon will strike a very deep note in your healthy spirit. Follow that music, keep your seventh and all your other chakras open and healthy, and listen.

In a healthy chakra system, the seventh chakra will close if it needs to shake off its dust and any old controlling cords or programming. You can identify a healthy seventh chakra vacation by the health of all the other chakras, especially the body/spirit connecting fourth, and the clairvoyant sixth. You will also have a lack of tension in your skull, and you'll be able to stay in the room in your head. Your aura and grounding cord will be strong and whole, even though your seventh chakra is closed right now.

Please give each of your chakras a congratulatory hello gift for doing such a good job that your seventh can take a rest. Place at least seven strongly grounded Sentries in front and in back of your seventh chakra for protection. You may allow your seventh to stay closed for up to a week. If it wants to stay off-line for a longer period of time, ask it why.

Often, your seventh chakra will need you to consciously examine your spiritual beliefs to see what fits and what doesn't. It is helpful at this point to burn a number of contracts with your spiritual or religious beliefs. After you perform a spiritual housecleaning, check in with your seventh chakra once again, and see if it is willing to open. If not, you may also need to beef up the upper portion of your aura, and to place many grounded Sentries in front of your seventh chakra to protect it against invalid belief systems.

When any chakra refuses to open back up, it can be a sign that someone in your life is still cording into it, and that you have not yet become sufficiently aware of the cording for your chakra to feel safe. Please sit and listen to your cautiously closed yet healthy seventh chakra. Perform a complete chakra reading and healing, and go over the special cording chapter later in this book.

TRAITS OF A HEALTHY SEVENTH CHAKRA: The seventh chakra contains the specific life purpose, spiritual path, healing information, and God-connection for each being. When the seventh chakra energy is allowed to flow, the highest level of spiritual knowledge, which is the knowledge of the self, is reached. When one truly knows and honors oneself, honor is conferred to all. Honor is given to life and to God. Honor is accorded to thoughts and to emotions, in their own time and in their own languages. The body and its needs are honored, and all parts of life are intrinsic to spiritual purpose.

When the seventh chakra is open in an unbalanced system, its energy can separate individuals from normal human interactions. When it is open in healthy and non-skewed systems, it makes one very much a part of life.

A healthy seventh chakra person can work, have money and children, drive a car, and eat, all while maintaining a spiritual path. They live in the world and in their bodies, but they maintain constant consciousness while they do. They have difficulties, because this is a difficult planet to live on. They get grumpy and sick, they may stomp and whine, but they stay on path. Healthy seventh chakra people keep doing their work. They make wonderful friends and lovers for people who want to do their own work, but because their very presence tends to shake up the psychic fabric around them, they often spend their lives alone.

In a healthy seventh chakra person, we see conflicting thoughts, strong emotions, human sexuality, a sense of humor, strong intuitive abilities, silliness, and divinity. In an unbalanced seventh chakra person, we would often see only the intuitive abilities and the divinity. This lack of balance trips over itself eventually, but usually only after hundreds of followers try to live the unbalanced life themselves while their unbalanced seventh chakra leader decays in some dramatic way.

You see, it's all about balance. Seventh chakra energy is very important, but if you try to have it all by itself, without the support of all the other chakra energies, you'll get into ungrounded, unsafe, inhuman trouble.

While you live in a body, you have real-time, real-life work to do. This work requires the support of all your skills, all your awareness, and all your chakras. The addition of healthy seventh chakra energy in a healthy, living, imperfect human body will make your real work beautiful, meaningful, funny, and possible. You will be spiritual *and* human. It can be done.

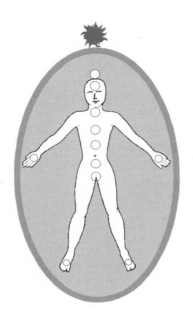

FURTHER INTO THE GARDEN

THE EIGHTH CHAKRA (THE GOLD SUN)

Your eighth chakra is a golden, sun-like energy center located above and outside of your aura. The Gold Sun chakra is not so much a gauge or container of specific abilities as it is an energy resource. Its function is to oversee the energies in your aura and your life. Your Gold Sun oversees all of you: your spiritual, mental, and emotional bodies, your physical body, your past, your present, and your future.

Your Gold Sun's specific ability is to cleanse and re-direct energy. It acts as a beacon for your own energy, which it cleanses of any attachments before making it available to you. Your Gold Sun also sorts the foreign energy you have picked up in images, messages, contracts, and cords (see the chapter on cording at the end of this book). Your Gold Sun can identify and cleanse foreign energy if you will take responsibility and ground the energy out of you.

Your Gold Sun is like a guardian angel or coach in your spiritual growth process. If you will trust and rely on it, your Gold Sun can help you heal any difficulty you have. By providing you with constantly available, cleansed energy, it can help you find the answer to any question. Your Gold Sun energy can help you find the solution to any problem. Your Gold Sun can also provide you with the energy to hurt yourself or others, if that is what you choose to do. Your Gold Sun chakra is an energy storehouse, and an energy clearinghouse. What you do with the energy it provides is your decision.

Because your Gold Sun lives outside of your aura, it is separate from your particular story and drama. It is dispassionate, unbiased, and neutral. Your Gold Sun won't withhold energy from you as a punishment, and it won't make more energy available as a reward. If you learn to manage your spiritual life in responsible ways, you will have more energy available. If you choose to squander your energy in attachments and addictions, you will have less energy. The condition of your Gold Sun chakra depends on you—on your treatment of yourself and others, and on your commitment to responsible spiritual communication.

The Gold Sun chakra exists in every person on the planet. Everyone has the opportunity to experience the flow of abundant, clean, and healing energy. Most people don't realize this opportunity exists.

I worked with the Gold Sun symbol for fifteen years before realizing it was the eighth chakra. I first thought it was just a nice visualization and centering device, but when I began to see the Gold Sun above all people, I knew it was real. Because of its neutrality, I guessed that it had something to do with spirit guides. I thought the Sun was a representation of each person's guiding information, but the golden energy was a puzzle. Golden energy has always symbolized Christ energy, whether the Christ being is Jesus, Buddha, Allah, or Horus. Over the years, I began to piece the puzzle together.

The Gold Sun chakra *is* Christ energy, spirit guide energy, and personal energy. It is the energetic container created for each of us by God. It is the superconscious, and it is the unconscious. The Gold Sun chakra can safely connect us to the larger world because it is separate from the shackles of the body, the personality, and the ravages of time.

When we call our energy back to us, or ground energy out of our territory, our Gold Sun chakra goes to work. It acts as a beacon, and a purifier for energy. The Gold Sun is the best chakra for this task, because it lives outside of the aura and the body. If any of the lower chakras attempts to pull stuck or foreign energies inside themselves, there will be trouble.

When unhealthy hand and heart chakras vacuum energy, they can cause chest, arm, hand, and neck pain. A third chakra that tries to vacuum up energy in its territory will create stomach distress first, and numerous problems later. A sponging second chakra can even lead the body into cancers and reproductive diseases. Too-receptive first or feet chakras will interfere with grounding, and may lead to uncontrolled *kundalini* rushes. None of the lower chakras have the time or space to cleanse and purify foreign energy.

A vacuuming heart chakra leads to runaway healing. An overly receptive fifth chakra can lead to schizophrenia, while a vacuuming sixth chakra can exhaust its owner with unending clairvoyant visions. An overly receptive seventh can lead to brain dysfunctions and seizure-disorders.

None of the body-linked chakras should vacuum energy. They're just not set up for it. The Gold Sun chakra can and does vacuum energy, because it was provided to us for that specific purpose. It is our prayer bank, our energy home, our link to God's energy, and our all-purpose energetic cleansing tool. The Gold Sun chakra is the energy that helps the aura and all the other chakras function. It is the energy that keeps us alive.

OPEN OR CLOSED EIGHTH CHAKRA

I have never seen a closed Gold Sun. I don't think it's possible to close this chakra. Our body-linked chakras are *supposed* to react to our strengths and our weaknesses. This is how we grow and learn. The Gold Sun, however, has to remain available to us at all times.

We can and do ignore our eighth chakra, but our eighth chakra always appears if we ask it to. I've seen less shiny suns in people who throw their energy away, but I've never seen a closed-down Gold Sun. Gold Suns are always open.

TRAITS OF A HEALTHY EIGHTH CHAKRA: I think this section should be called "Traits of a Person who Pays Attention to His Gold Sun." The Gold Sun chakra, even when it's pretty dim, can brighten up in minutes when people sit and ground. There's no real trick to healing a Gold Sun chakra. You just have to pay attention to it.

If you stay in contact with your Gold Sun chakra, you will have all the knowledge you need. You'll have all the healing information, all the laughter, all the self-love, all the forgiveness, all the emotions, and everything else. When you are connected to the wealth of your Gold Sun, you'll have more energy than you could ever use, more true riches than you could ever dream of, and more opportunities than you could possibly undertake. With this kind of back-up, it's a cinch to be of service to the world. With this kind of back-up, your service will be inestimable.

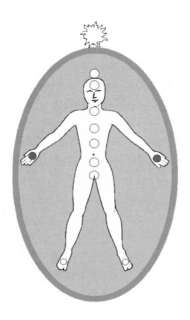

FURTHER INTO THE GARDEN

THE HAND CHAKRAS

In the center of each of the palms are the hand chakras, which can be either expressive or receptive, depending on the circumstance. During a healing or artistic expression, the hand chakras will channel energy from within the body or from a healing guide out into the world. During periods of intense study, lovemaking, or meditation, the hands can channel external energy and information into the body.

If you have lost one or both of your hands, this topic still pertains to you. Though your physical hands may be gone, your energy hands, and your hand chakras, are still alive and active. Read on.

The hand chakras are not exactly like the seven major body-linked chakras. They are naturally smaller in size (about two to three inches in diameter when open), they open and close more often than the major chakras, and they do not have a particular color. The hand chakras are channels through which many energies may flow. They are not specific storehouses of specific energy. The hand chakras are connected to the heart chakra, and their general condition shows us where we are in our ability to give and receive and create in the world.

There is a difference between the functioning of the heart and the hands. The heart chakras condition relates to our ability to channel internal love and artistic information throughout our body and spirit. The hand chakra's condition speaks to our ability to channel love and artistry in the external world.

In situations of person-to-person healing or lovemaking, or deep creative expression, the heart chakra will send its energy down through the arms and out the hand chakras. This flow can be very healing, unless the heart chakra is overstimulated or unaware, and spends too much time draining itself in this fashion. Without a conscious connection from the heart to the hands, the heart chakra may become misshapen as it tries to pour itself out and down the arms. When the hands and heart are properly connected, the outward flow of heart energy can be controlled by the hands. A method for connecting the heart and hands is included in this chapter.

As with the *kundalini* rush, a little bit of overflowing heart chakra energy goes a long way. Overflowing heart chakra energy leads to the runaway healing we talked about in *Rebuilding the Garden*. If this pouring-out tendency is not corrected, the heart chakra will become exhausted, and the spirit/body split will re-emerge. Physical and emotional exhaustion will soon follow. Reading and healing the heart chakra will pull its energy back to center once again, as will connecting the hands and heart consciously.

The hand chakras are used most actively by massage therapists and intuitive healers, who in many cases, don't have the training or understanding to keep their hand chakras healthy. I see many cases of hand, wrist, elbow, and shoulder problems in such people. This can of course be attributed to overwork, and the improper use of the muscles. But, it can also be a sign that the healer is pouring too much heart chakra energy out of himself, or allowing his client's energy to flow into his hands and up into his body.

Healers are not the only people who are troubled by hand-chakra malfunctions. House-cleaners, executive secretaries, elementary school teachers, and counselors of all kinds will very often vacuum up the distress around them as they clean up, or type memos, or place their hands on people. Symptoms of hand chakra vacuuming will include hand and arm pain (including carpal tunnel), shoulder stiffness, weakness in the arms and upper back, and pain in the region of the heart.

The body doesn't like to be filled with other people's energy, attention, problems, and wishes. It will react with pain and dysfunction, because it knows that its own needs are always pushed aside when other people's problems are brought inside it.

If your hand chakras have learned the bad habit of empathetic sponging (see the chapter on the second chakra), your body has probably been complaining about it for a while. Apologize, learn the correct method of heart-to-hand connection, and break the habit. A healthy and aware method of hand chakra healing, for the self and for others, is included the chapter on the Chakra Reading. For now, please go over the warning signals of unbalanced hand chakras.

OPEN OR CLOSED HAND CHAKRAS

The hand chakras open and close all the time, and change their degree of openness moment by moment. They are very much more active in this respect than the seven major body-linked chakras.

If your chakra system is fairly aligned and healthy, but your hand chakras are wide open or shut tight, rub your hands together briskly. The hand chakras may change size. Rubbing the hands brings energy to these chakras and often pulls them into present time. During a reading or Chakra Check, the hands should be open to two or three inches in diameter and ready to work. If, after rubbing them briskly, they're not ready or willing to open to your specifications, read on.

Constantly open hand chakras in an unhealthy chakra system can affect the joints and muscles of the hands by making them weaker than usual. The hands in this system will be unable to grasp and hold onto things. Essentially, all the energy that should be in the hands is pouring out of them. This weakens the hands.

People with clumsy hands, or hands that are constantly being bumped, scraped, banged, and burned generally have their hand chakras far too open for health and safety. This weakened state of the hands often accompanies a wide-open, runaway-healing heart chakra.

Open hand chakras are necessary during a specific task such as healing or creating art, but they have to be able to close back down. If your training has placed an overemphasis on the heart chakra attributes of healing and the giving of unconditional love, your hand chakras may be open and pouring out heart chakra energy twenty-four hours a day. If this is the case, the heart chakra will usually be flattened out into a horizontal oblong shape instead of a healthy, rounded circle. The heart chakra in this situation actually looks as if it's starting to drain out into the arms.

We've already talked about closing down a runaway heart chakra. Work with the hand chakras is also vital, and tremendously supportive in bringing the heart back to a place of balance in a functioning chakra system. Working with the hand chakras, which you can close by simply making a fist, blocks off a traditional avenue of heart energy drainage.

When your hand chakras are closed, your heart energy has to stay in your body. This may be uncomfortable at first, especially if your sense of self is completely based on your ability to love and heal others. You may not know what to do with your own healing energy. You may not know how to give to yourself. You may not even want to. Do it anyway.

Give to yourself by taking it easy, by feeding yourself handmade foods, by taking time for yourself, by saying no to half of the demands on your time, and by checking into the room in your head. Set aside a time each day to do whatever your little one likes to do, no matter how silly it is.

Take time out to color in a coloring book, buy a goofy shirt, play with a puppy, or go to the zoo. Lighten up and have a little fun, and place your hands right over your heart when you feel the need to ignore yourself and barrel headlong into a one-sided healing relationship. Take your life into your own hands.

Open hand chakras can also be in the vacuum mode, as opposed to the draining mode explained above. When the hand chakras are vacuuming energy into the body, the heart chakra will not be spread out and elongated. The heart in this case will usually be rather small and bright, and it may have squared-off, as opposed to rounded boundary edges. In any chakra, geometric outer edges often signal distress. You will find corners and angles on chakras trying to keep their energy protected from incorrect belief systems that interfere with their functioning.

A squared-off or geometric chakra is trying to deflect incoming energy by presenting sharp angles instead of welcoming curves. A heart that is trapped between two unaware, vacuuming hand chakras will become defended, as it should. Physical symptoms will include upper back pain or distress, breathing problems, and all sorts of digestive disturbances as the third chakra tries to step in and protect the heart.

A vacuuming hand chakra healer will also experience burnout during or after their healing, cleaning, organizing, or counseling sessions. They will require a great deal of rest. Essentially, a vacuuming hand chakra healer is a sponge healer who will soon break down. The correct heart-to-hand connection technique taught in this chapter can help heal such healers.

Constantly closed hand chakras can stiffen and swell the joints and muscles of the hands. This is a sign that a person's ability to give and create is stunted and somewhat arthritic. If your hand chakras are shut tight, the normal flow of energy through your body will be negatively affected. You'll be clogged up. If you can't paint a little picture or play chopsticks on the piano, please find some way to create a flow in your hands. Our society places such impossible requirements on artistic and creative expression that it is a wonder anyone wants to love, paint, dance, or create. Still, many people take to the challenge. You can, too.

You can bake or cook something by hand, clean and restore some piece of furniture or automotive gear, give someone a shoulder rub or haircut, do Tai Chi or Yoga, or spend some time petting an animal. Concentrate on learning to connect your heart and your hands in healthy ways. Get your energy flowing again, please. A heart-to-hand connection and healing is included in this chapter. If your hand chakras have been closed, please perform this healing at least twice a day until you re-establish the flow.

Hand chakras can also take healthy chakra vacations. But, because they are in use so much of the time, it is highly unusual for them to go off-line for more than a day or two. You can identify a healthy hand-chakra vacation by the health and circular shape of your heart chakra, and by the feeling of relaxation and grace in your arms, hands and fingers, even though your hand chakras are closed.

Hand chakras go off-line when new information about healthy healing and self-love is being processed. The hands close off in order to keep the heart chakra energy in the body. They shut down to help you step out of the healer-giver role for a while. Hand chakras, however, need to be available to you. Please check in on them two or three times a day while they are closed. Give all your other chakras, especially your heart chakra, congratulatory hello gifts. When any of your chakras can take a vacation, your system is doing well. Let each of your chakras know you appreciate their balance and their communication skills.

For the hands themselves, please cover them with a glove of grounded Sentries, and ask them to show you what energy support they would need to open again. They will usually describe it manually. Watch and learn.

TRAITS OF HEALTHY HAND CHAKRAS: People with healthy hand chakras can translate the information of their healthy chakra system, and get it out into the world. They are naturally (as opposed to compulsively) giving and caring, but they have an extra dimension: they can also receive. They can receive help, compliments, gifts, and loving advice without losing their center, and they can give all these things to others without creating indebtedness, guilt, or recriminations.

Healthy hand chakras confer a natural creativity to a person, whether they are "artists" or not. Such people's creativity will flow, and they will not suffer from dramatic artistic blocks or fallow periods. They will have a flair for dressing or cooking or home decoration or car restoration—whatever makes them happy—and they will not need to rely on teachers or institutions to validate their artistic expression. They will have a comfortable give-and-take relationship with the world and the people around them. They will also have a comfortable give-and-take relationship with their own energy. They will be able to protect their giving nature by closing off their heart-to-hand connection in the presence of habitually needy people.

CONNECTING THE HAND CHAKRAS TO THE HEART CHAKRA

The hands and heart are usually connected in most people. It is always a good idea, though, to check in on the quality of that connection, especially in cases where the heart chakra is troubled or misshapen, or the hands and arms are stiff, cramped, weakened, or accident-prone.

The connection between the hands and the heart begins with a healthy heart chakra. The healing of the heart is the first step in this process.

When you are centered and in your head, please envision your heart chakra as a circular, emerald-green energy center between three to five inches in diameter. Now, envision each of your hand chakras in the center of the rounded depression in your palms as circular and open as well.

As you remain seated comfortably behind your eyes, envision a portion of the emerald energy in your heart chakra moving up toward each of your shoulders. Be sure that your heart chakra remains circular and normally sized. Know that you are not draining the energy out of your heart, but simply redirecting some of its inexhaustible supply.

See the emerald energy of your heart chakra moving up into your shoulders and then down into each of your arms. Feel your heart chakra energy as it moves gently through the bone marrow of your upper arms and through to your elbows and lower arms. Watch from inside your head as your heart chakra energy moves down through your wrists and flows out of each of your hand chakras, pushing any energy blockages in front of it.

When your hand chakras are connected to your heart chakra, you should be able to feel an increased heat or pressure in your hands. If you can't, you may have a clog somewhere in your arms or hands.

To release the clog, bring your palms together and rub them briskly until you can feel heat inside both of your hands. Now, let your arms hang down, and feel their tingling heaviness. This is the feeling you will be aiming for when your heart energy is flowing into your hand chakras.

Bring your hands together and rub them briskly again. When they are warm, use them to actually move your heart chakra energy out into your arms.

Place your right hand a few inches in front of your heart chakra, and describe a small circle over it, as if you are stirring the heart chakra energy. Use your right hand to bring some of the heart's green energy out and up to your left shoulder. Gently move a portion of your heart chakra energy out and down your left arm.

When you get down to your left palm, use your right hand to describe a circle around that hand chakra, and see your hand chakra filled with flowing green heart energy.

When your left-hand connection is made, drop your right hand. Use your left to bring your heart chakra energy into your right hand. You may need to establish this connection a few times each day if you are an unconscious vacuum healer, but this connection will soon begin to flow on its own.

Open your eyes and move your hands and arms around. Open and close your palms and feel the difference in heart-energy flow as you do. Place your open hands onto any uncomfortable places in your body, and you can perform a small heart-chakra healing on yourself. Place your open hands over your heart chakra, and you can close this energy circuit and give love to yourself when your heart falls out of balance.

Maintain this heart-hand connection at all times. Be aware, if runaway healing is part of your past, that you don't allow heart energy to rush out of your hands in unconscious ways, and that you don't start vacuuming up the energy around you. When your heart is connected consciously to your hands, and you have control and awareness of your heart energy, runaway healing and hand sponging are far less likely; however, they can still be done. Please re-read the warning signals of too-open hand chakras, and the chapter on the sponge-healing second chakra if you fall backward into old relating styles.

If you have trouble keeping your healing energy in your own body, place your open hands over your heart each morning and evening for about a month. If you feel your heart *going out* to another person who has not specifically asked you for a healing, place your hands over your heart immediately. Close the circuit and remind yourself that everyone has their own healing energy. You don't have to heal the world right now. This is the time for you.

Now that you know how to connect heart and hands, please look in on their connection each time you do a Chakra Check or reading, and every time you perform a Gold Sun healing. Do not let your heart chakra flatten out into a horizontal oblong as it tries to pour itself down your arms. The hand-connected heart chakra should remain healthy and circular, just as the first chakra remains healthy and circular even though a portion of its energy is directed downward as a grounding cord.

Also, do not allow your hands to vacuum energy in unconscious ways. This will only create havoc in your heart chakra and your chakra system as a whole. Instead, learn the heart-and-hand chakra healing method outlined in the chapter on the Chakra Reading. Stop hurting yourself.

Take some time to establish a strong heart-to-hand connection. We will rely on this connection in the chakra readings and healings to come.

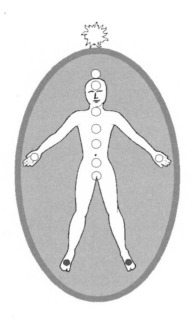

THE FEET CHAKRAS

Both feet have chakras in the center of their arches. Like the hand chakras, the feet chakras can be either expressive or receptive in nature. During grounding and exercise, the feet chakras help the body to channel energy downward into the earth. During walking meditations or nature excursions, the feet chakras will open to allow earth energy to come up into the body.

If you are missing one or both of your feet, this topic still applies to you. Though your physical feet may be gone, your energy body still has legs, feet, and feet chakras. Keep reading.

The health of the feet chakras relates not just to our ability to be in the body and grounded, but to our ability to act on the planet in real time as grounded, in-body spirits. This is an important distinction. It is quite possible to be in the head and grounded from the first chakra without really connecting to the earth, especially if the third, fourth, and fifth chakras are not able to communicate with one another as they should.

If the important spirit/body communication is blocked in chakras three, four, or five, the spirit and body will not have a clean connection. The grounding abilities, which are a sign of spirit/body agreement, will be more of an intellectual ideal than a hands-on (or feets-on) reality. By looking at your feet chakras and their connection to your first chakra, you can find out if your grounding is as strong and real as it could be.

The feet chakras, like the hand chakras, open and close at will in response to the body's need for earth connection or earth energy. They too are smaller than the central chakras, sizing in at two to three inches in diameter when open. The feet chakras do not have a specific color, but they are oftentimes shades of brown, like the brownish tinge of earth energy, or red if they are connected to the energy of the first chakra.

When grounding and body-connection are strong in an individual, some of his first chakra energy will flow down the center of his legs (inside the marrow, usually) and out through his feet chakras. This flow means that the first chakra is healthy—that its functions are not conceptual, but actual.

When the heart energy flows from the hands, you see concrete examples of self-and-other-love and healing, even if that connection is not yet conscious. When the first chakra energy flows from the feet, you see concrete examples of grounding, earthiness, and the spirit-body connection.

Healthy feet chakras create and nourish a connection to the wise, calm energy that lives inside the earth. The feet chakras connect us to nature by opening to allow earth energy to come into our bodies to cleanse, center, and ground us. The feet chakras also give us the chance to off-load any stress, fatigue, or disharmony in our bodies by opening to allow our excess energy to drain into the accepting, cleansing soil.

When the feet chakras are working, any movement of the lower body is grounding. Walking, dancing, housecleaning, and pushing a shopping cart all become spiritual grounding exercises when the feet are allowed to maintain a constant, give-and-take contact with the earth.

OPEN OR CLOSED FEET CHAKRAS

Very open feet chakras in an unhealthy system are an emergency grounding tool. If you are out of balance and ungrounded, but your feet still try to keep you connected to the grounding qualities of earth energy by staying very open, consider yourself lucky.

Though it's important to heal and align all of your chakras as soon as you can, it is also important to congratulate your open feet chakras for doing the right thing! If your feet chakras try to keep you grounded even when you're not helping, you've got a very evolved and responsible body. Treat it with love and care. Evolved bodies have a hell of a time in this noisy, unhealthy society, especially if their owner (you) ignores them!

As you go through the full chakra healing in response to your too-open feet chakras, pay special attention to the connections between your third, fourth, and fifth chakras. Their body/spirit agreements or arguments are usually a mitigating factor in any grounding blockages. Also, when you get to your first chakra, please see a portion of its ruby red energy flowing down the center of the bones in your legs, straight through to your feet chakras. This connection will help calm and re-size your feet chakras so that they can relax a little. If you need a bit of visual help in re-sizing these chakras, envision the closing mechanism of a camera shutter.

At the end of your full chakra healing, take extra time in the chapter called *The Gold Sun Healing for Chakras*. Establish a good flow of golden energy throughout your pelvis, hips, thighs, knees, calves, ankles, and feet. These areas may need extra attention for a while. It would be wise to do a Gold Sun healing daily until the flow of energy from your first chakra to your feet chakras is easy to maintain.

Unhealthy, open feet chakras can create physical problems, such as clumsiness, constant toe-stubbing, or the tendency to sprain ankles and knees. Once the healing flow of energy is re-established, and the feet are re-attached to the consciousness, these difficulties should subside.

Wide-open feet chakras in a healthy chakra system are a sign that the body is re-acquainting itself with the wisdom and healing of earth energy. Though many people feel that true guidance comes only from above—from the cosmic, spiritual realm—real wisdom comes from a balance of earth energy *and* cosmic energy.

Cosmic energy makes for a well-balanced spirit, and earth energy makes for a well-balanced body in which the spirit can live. Though cosmic energy is generally given more importance, physical balance is vital in these ungrounded times. Wide-open feet chakras in a healthy chakra system are gathering wisdom and guidance on how to attune the body to the rhythms, cycles, and energies of the planet. This information will bring much healing insight to each of the central chakras.

Though we usually want any wide-open chakras closed within a week, the feet chakras and earth energy may need more time to establish their healing connection. Since the earth works in cycles and seasons and real time, it may need more real time to fully involve the body in a particular lesson or healing modality. Let it. Maintain the health and alignment of your central chakras. Meditate regularly to support your chakra system while your feet chakras participate in this earthy healing.

It is a good idea, when the feet chakras are opening to new information, to sit and practice your meditation and healing at the same time and in the same place each day. Earth energy is very responsive to time, place, and stability. When you center yourself on a regular and dedicated schedule, the earth energy will be able to align itself to your schedule, and offer healing information to you as you meditate. Listen and learn. Earth energy is infinitely healing and infinitely wise.

Closed feet chakras in an unhealthy system are signs of an unwillingness to ground and connect with the earth. The closing can also be a symptom of the feet chakra's response to first chakra molest contracts, cording, and damage (see the special chapter on cording later in this book).

The feet chakras can also be closed because the body is not getting enough gentle, reasonable daily exercise to keep its energy flowing. I say gentle and reasonable because many exercise addicts have closed feet chakras and are prone to constant lower-body injuries. Compulsive exercising is a very ungrounding act, because it ignores normal bodily signals such as pain, hunger, fatigue, and plain old common sense. If you are a no-pain-no-gain type of macho workout person with grounding trouble and closed feet chakras, lighten up. You don't have to stop exercising, but you do have to learn to listen to your body instead of forcing it to do so many miles or reps or whatever. Getting into contact with your body and your feet chakras will help you listen.

Closed feet chakras can make the feet and legs feel very tight, inflexible, and possibly arthritic. The feet and legs may even show signs of vascular insufficiency because energy does not flow through them properly. There may also be wide temperature swings in the feet as the body tries to respond to this lack of energy.

I also see closed feet chakras in people I call "seventh chakra fairies" (myself, at times, included). Seventh chakra fairies are people whose body/spirit skew is decidedly spirit-sided. They are often filled with spiritual information, intuition, and guidance, while their bodies, their homes, and their finances are in a complete shambles. Interestingly, many spiritual teachings have downplayed the importance of the physical world (calling it an illusion), precisely because so few of their spirit-skewed disciples could function within it.

Let's not kid ourselves. We are spirits in bodies, and our whole purpose in incarnating was to learn to live in and communicate with the body and the physical world. Travelling in the astral realm, receiving higher guidance, communing with the spirits and so forth—these are nice things to do, but without grounding, they can create or intensify a whopping body/spirit split.

When seventh chakra fairies come to me and ask for spiritual guidance, or astral travel tips, I ask them how their legs feel. I ask them about their hair, their stomach, their car, and their finances. I get disjointed and unsure answers, because common, everyday life is uncomfortable and even unknown to these people. They often have no idea about how they feel, what they want, where they're going in the world, or how to get there. But they want to learn to do more astral travel.

I will tell you what I tell them: as soon as you fall asleep, you can astral travel to your heart's delight and be one with all the spirits. While you are awake and alive, be awake and alive, and get into your body. You can only ascend to spirit after you do your work on this planet properly, which means in an in-body way. If you over-emphasize the spiritual side of life and ignore your body, no matter how exalted you become, you will have to come back into another body because you did not take care of this one.

When you get into your body and get grounded, your spirituality will have a depth of meaning unavailable to seventh chakra fairies. When you allow your feet chakras to connect you to the earth and all its incredible wisdom, your body will become not only a healthy, aware organism, but a true temple of spirit as well.

As with other healthy chakras, the feet can close off for a vacation every now and then. You will know this vacation by the health of your first and second chakras, and by a loose, relaxed and lively feeling in your pelvis, legs, and feet, even though your feet chakras are closed.

The feet will go off line, usually for no more than a day or two, when new information about grounding and earth-connection is being processed. If the feet chakras stay closed for more than two days, their absence could create imbalances in grounding for once-split people. It is wise to check in on them throughout their vacation days, and to enclose your feet in grounded Sentry socks.

If your feet chakras are still on vacation after two days, please perform a complete chakra reading. Re-establish the flow of energy from your first chakra down to your feet chakras (with the connection technique at the end of this chapter). Ask your feet chakras what energy or real-life support they would require to open back up. Often, they will ask you to commit to daily leg movement such as walking or biking. Do it.

TRAITS OF HEALTHY FEET CHAKRAS: When the feet chakras are working at their optimum level, they make grounding second nature. They connect us to the information, energy, and healing qualities of the earth, and they help our bodies feel more real. Reasonable exercise, proper diet, peaceful living and working situations, and effortless health-building are all external signs of a close and healing internal connection with the planet.

Healthy feet chakras confer a centered, stable, grounded, yet deeply spiritual energy to their owners, very much like the energy of nature-centered tribal people. When the body holds its honorable position as the arbiter between earth and sky, all its movements on the planet are a part of the movement of its spirit, and vice versa. Healthy feet chakras, and the planetary connection they provide, help to make this balance possible

Sometimes, healthy feet chakras can make the body feel almost draggy, as if gravity exerts more force on it than on other people's bodies. This happens when people with healthy feet chakras head toward a spirit/body split. The heaviness in the feet is in direct proportion to the over-emphasis on cosmic spiritual information.

When your legs or pelvis begin to feel dragged down, it doesn't mean you are grounding *too much*. It means that you are heading for a spirit/body split again, and are most likely grounding *too little*. Congratulate yourself—you are the owner of healthy and responsible feet chakras. Pay attention, get in your body, and perform this new healing.

CONNECTING THE FEET CHAKRAS TO THE FIRST CHAKRA

In naturally grounded people, the feet chakras connect themselves to the healing energy of the earth without any assistance. In split people, the feet chakras are generally cut off from the healing energy of the earth. This lack of connection makes grounding and living in a body very difficult.

When the first chakra energy can be channelled through the legs and down to the feet chakras, the legs themselves become a grounding tool. Connecting the first chakra and the feet chakras makes walking and exercising a meditative process. Each time the legs move and the feet touch the ground, the connection to the earth is re-established. When the feet chakras are connected and healthy, and the simple movements of the body provide grounding, the body and spirit communicate more easily with one another.

As with the heart-to-hand connection, the first-to-feet connection begins with a healthy first chakra. By this time, your first chakra should be fairly healthy if you have maintained your grounding cord. If it is not, please study any deviations in your first chakra, and heal it before you attempt to connect it to your feet chakras. If your first chakra energy is blasting upward, please go to the *Kundalini* Healing in *Rebuilding the Garden* and then perform an entire chakra system healing before you go on.

When you are centered and in your head, envision your first chakra as a healthy, circular, ruby-red energy center. See the clear and strong attachment between it and your grounding cord. Now, envision the chakras in the insteps of each of your feet. See them as open and circular.

From inside the room in your head, allow a portion of your red first chakra energy to flow outward to each of your thighs. See the red energy travelling from each side of your still-circular first chakra down through the marrow of your thighs. Watch the energy continue down through your knees and calves. Know that you are not draining your first chakra, but just redirecting some of its inexhaustible energy.

Stay centered and in your head, and watch as the red first chakra energy travels down into your ankles and then out of the chakras in the insteps of each of your feet. Feel the energy moving through your legs and down into the earth.

If the feeling of being connected to the earth is very unusual, or if your legs feel hot or heavy, you can bet that your feet chakras were not previously in use. If you experience only slight changes, your feet chakras were probably working well on their own. Now, attach a grounding cord to each of your feet chakras, and you're done!

If you're having a lot of trouble making this connection, please use your heart-connected hands to help move the first chakra energy out and down your legs. When you get to each of your feet, use your hands to describe circles over your feet chakras. Feel yourself stirring up their energy. This will often wake up your feet chakras and get them ready to work.

You may need to use your hands to move this energy from your first chakra to your feet chakras a number of times. This is a normal occurrence at first. In time, your first-to-feet connection will be effortless.

Please maintain a constant awareness of the connection between your first chakra and your feet chakras, especially if you have had trouble grounding in the past. This connection will help to clear out the energy trapped in your lower body, which will make both grounding and the removal of molest contracts easier.

When you have initiated this conscious connection between your first chakra and your feet chakras, your connection to the earth will be much more secure. From this point on, please check in on this connection every time you perform a Chakra Check, a chakra reading, or a Gold Sun healing.

Many Gardeners find that this first-to-feet connection can be substituted for the first chakra grounding cord. If you can maintain your grounding better this way, please feel free to drop your first chakra grounding cord, and ground through your feet instead. It's actually a more natural way to ground, once you've got your first chakra cleared of old abuse energy.

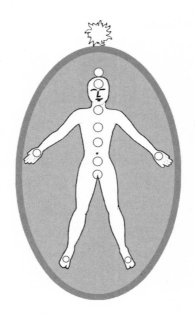

FURTHER INTO THE GARDEN

THE CHAKRA READING

After you've done a Chakra Check and are in a clear, grounded, in-your-head meditative posture, you can revisit each chakra, starting at your seventh chakra and working your way down.

During the Chakra Check, you told your chakras how they were supposed to look. During your chakra reading, you will now listen or watch to see how they *do* look.

Your chakra reading will start out just like a Chakra Check. You will first place an image of an ideal chakra over your own, and then you will be receptive to any changes your chakra shows you.

After you put up your picture of what your Chakra-Checked chakra *should* look like, you make room for what it *does* look like.

This is the technique most beginning psychics use to clear their thoughts and release their preconceptions: they place an image of what they think should happen, or what they think they know about their client, and then sit and wait for changes. When the changes are received, the reading begins. Psychics who cannot be honest about their preconceptions usually give readings tainted with their own prejudices.

Many new readers are confused by this, and will tell me, "I can't get the hang of this! My seventh chakra doesn't look anything like it should. I give up!" They think real psychics know everything right away, have perfect chakras, and are all-powerful. Wrong!

Good psychics aren't cocky know-it-alls. They go into readings ready to find out what they *don't* know! Therefore, those confused and upset early readers are already well on their way to competence. They find out right away that they don't know everything.

When chakras don't respond to perfect Chakra Check images, they are ready for a reading and healing right now. These chakras don't want to waste any time; they exhibit their changes and deviations immediately! The changes chakras display can be dramatic in terms of shape, size, and color. Or, the changes can be very minor, such as the chakra exhibiting a lighter shade than the color placed there during the Chakra Check.

Do not consider yourself un-intuitive if you find no changes. You may be lucky enough to have a very healthy set of chakras that don't show any signs of damage or disruption. Your system may be so willing to be healthy that your simple Chakra Check was all it needed to get back on track. Good. All you really need to do is to go on to the Gold Sun healing for chakras that comes up in the next chapter, and you're done!

As you read each of your seven central chakras, be aware of: their size and shape (they should have circular edges and be between three to five inches in diameter); their size and alignment in relation to one another (they should all be roughly the same size and in a straight line up the front of the body); the purity of their color (their colors should be clear and distinct from one another); and the completeness of their edges (which should be without tears, holes, bulges, or thin spots). Each chakra's energy should also be moving or swirling freely.

As you check in with your hand and feet chakras, be aware that their normal size is between two and three inches in diameter. These chakras have no regular color, though the feet chakras can be red if they are connected to the energy of the first chakra, or brownish-green if they are connected to the earth. The hand chakras may be gold, or heart-chakra green if they are connected to the heart.

Both the hand and feet chakras should be circular, with distinct edges free of holes, tears, or hazy sections.

Start your reading at your seventh (or crown) chakra and work your way down to your first chakra. Read your hand chakras along with your heart chakra, and read your feet chakras along with your first chakra.

To read your chakras, place a Chakra Check picture of how you think each chakra should look, and then be open to any changes you may perceive. If you find changes and deviations from the Chakra Check norm, look up the possible meanings below, or let your chakra tell you what's wrong with it.

When you finish reading each chakra, please send it another Chakra Check picture of itself at its healthiest, and move down to the next chakra.

If you need to, you can use your hands to mold your chakras into the correct size and shape, and to stir their energy with your fingers before you move on. When all of your chakras have been read and attended to, and your hands and feet are attached to their respective central chakras, you can perform the special heart-and-hand chakra healing which is taught at the end of this chapter. Then, all that's left is to perform the special Gold Sun healing for chakras in the next chapter.

This reading process may seem rather involved, and it certainly can be, but this longer chakra reading is not meant to be a daily occurrence. At first, you may want to read your chakras regularly, but you don't need to. A very quick Chakra Check a few times a week is usually sufficient once all the chakras are in line with one another. Longer chakra readings should be saved for times of transition or stress. When I teach, I perform chakra readings on myself weekly, but during regular life, I generally go two-to-three months between readings.

WHAT TO DO ABOUT PROBLEMS IN YOUR CHAKRAS

Though we are now going to take a look at the meanings of chakra deviations, all chakra problems can be healed by placing a Chakra Check picture of each chakra at its healthiest over the injured chakra. Any deviation that does not immediately respond to your healing may simply need to be there for a while.

Don't invalidate your healing abilities or pour grunting, sweaty effort at your chakra's problems. Each chakra is alive and aware. Chakras naturally know what they are doing, and if you'll simply allow them to communicate with each other, they'll pull themselves together.

The most healing thing you can do for your chakras is to be aware of and responsive to their messages. Keep your meditation and healing skills alive and active so that your energy body is in general good health most of the time. Chakras do not need you to poke and peer at them; they only need gentle attention and a little direction.

If an injured chakra does not respond to your suggestions, let it be, place a Chakra Check picture of it at its healthiest over it, and go on to the next chakra. After you finish reading all of your chakras, you can run a bit of healing heart chakra energy through each of your chakras (a technique taught in this chapter). After that, the Gold Sun healing for chakras will help them come into alignment and into present time. This will supply all the healing energy your chakras need.

Do another full reading in a day or two, and you will see the changes your chakra system has made on its own. If your system is exactly as injured as before, with no changes whatsoever, that may be a sign of cording energy (which you can read about at the end of this book), or drug damage.

Please, if you are at all serious about becoming spiritually aware, clean the drugs out of your body and give your poor energy tools a rest. Drugs and alcohol will create tremendous damage and chaos in your chakras, but the damage can be alleviated if you clean out now. A good acupuncturist/Chinese herbalist can not only help you detoxify, but can help re-balance your energy field so that you can begin to work with and use it again. Otherwise, you'll just spend all your healing and meditation time putting out the fires that drugs cause, instead of moving forward in ability, awareness, and strength.

Now, on to the deviations you may see in your chakras.

CHAKRA DEVIATIONS

ALIGNMENT: The seven central chakras should be lined up both vertically and laterally—all facing forward from the centerline of the body. When the chakras are out of alignment, they are also out of contact with one another.

Sometimes, the chakras will edge away from centerline if the system as a whole is heavily corded, and therefore filled with unhealthy and unworkable information. The chakras will not stack on top of one another in a straight vertical line—they will appear crooked and off-kilter.

In a corded and unbalanced system, the chakras will try to move away from the main channel of energy so that they can function on their own to some extent. This left-or-right-sided deviation can be healed easily in the special Gold Sun healing for chakras that follows, and through the cord-removal process at the end of this book. However, it is also a good idea to check in on left-right deviations in a philosophical way.

For some people, the aspects particular to each chakra exist in one gender only. Women can be fourth-chakra empathic, but men can't; men can be first-chakra sexual, but women aren't allowed; women can have sixth-chakra intuition, but men can only have facts, and so on. We know that all of this is silly, but check it out: are your receptive "feminine" chakras (2, 4, & 6) drifting to the left while your expressive "masculine" chakras (1, 3, 5, & 7) drift to the right? If they are, take another look at the chapter on the second chakra and gender skews. Pull your chakras back to center, please.

In another type of alignment deviation, the chakras will line up vertically, but will not face forward as they should. Instead, these chakras face up, or down. This deviation usually occurs in people with a long-standing, ungrounded body/spirit split. These people's chakras will face downward to seek grounding and earth energy, or they will face upward, seeking spiritual information and guidance.

Sometimes, the chakras maintain a central alignment, but look off to the left or the right if they are depending on the teachings of an authority figure or guru for their sense of well-being. A person with this deviation will usually be out of body, with very little belief in his or her own healing abilities. Because the chakras seek safety and information, they will try to reach out and connect themselves with some external authority figure, with very little lasting success.

In all cases of alignment problems, the chakras need to be moved gently back to center, facing forward. This can be accomplished in the Gold Sun healing for chakras; however, the earlier skills of grounding, staying in the center of the head, and defining the aura must also be revisited.

If the chakras are out of line because of cord interference, it is also important to review contract burning, the Gold Sun healing for chakras that follows this chapter, and the chapter on cords at the end of this book.

COLOR: When you find a different color in your chakra than the one you placed there during your Chakra Check, your chakra system is sending you a message. To help you decipher that message, I am reproducing the color guide from *Rebuilding the*

Garden. Still, I must warn you that the interpretation of color is completely subjective. Your senses, feelings, and ideas about color will always be more appropriate for you than mine will. Trust yourself.

Before we go to general colors though, there is a very specific color deviation (which I call an *assist*) that should be examined. If you find the color of another chakra in the one you are currently reading, congratulate yourself. You are the owner of a very healthy and communicative chakra system.

Sometimes, when one chakra closes down or becomes unhealthy, and your chakra system is aligned and aware, a nearby, healthy chakra will lend a part of its energy to the ailing chakra. Unlike a *kundalini* rush, in which the first chakra rather ham-handedly blasts its energy through all the upper chakras, an assist is a very directed, partial or complete color wash that is specific to the injured chakra.

For instance: if a person is having a terrible time communicating his intuitive knowledge, the connection between his clairvoyant sixth chakra and his communicative fifth chakra may weaken. The fifth chakra may even lose energy and threaten to close or go dark as his communication skills lie fallow. Oftentimes, the third, fourth, or seventh chakras will become aware of the problem. One of them will send a portion of its own energy into the ailing throat chakra. This assistance will help to keep the throat chakra going until the crisis is over. In such a case, you would find third chakra yellow, heart chakra green, or seventh chakra violet in this person's normally blue fifth chakra.

This conscious color-lending—this assist—between chakras usually means that the sending chakra is healthy, and that the chakra system is balanced, aware, and inventive. In a healthy system, the chakras communicate with and look out for one another.

When you find a color assist, congratulate each of your chakras for doing such good work. Then, ground the assisting color out of the ailing chakra as you place the correct color in. Clear out the areas behind and in front of the ailing chakra (with Velcro wands from *Rebuilding the Garden*) so that whatever was in the ailing chakra's way can be grounded out and redirected. This doesn't take a lot of work. As I said, a chakra system that is aware enough to perform an assist is healthy enough to get back into shape with only a minimum of spiritual healing.

Usually, an assist is a good sign unless the assisting chakra is more than three chakras away from the unhealthy one. If I see red first chakra energy in an ailing heart chakra, I want to know why the second and third chakras didn't notice the problem, and what the heck is going on with them. Or, if I see violet seventh chakra energy in an ailing second chakra, I want to know what chakras three through six have been doing in their spare time.

A general rule is this: an assist should be done by a nearby chakra. If it's not, the chakra system may not be aligned or healthy. In many cases, this situation can even signal that only one or two chakras are functioning, and that these few strong chakras may be overburdened by taking responsibility for all the other weak ones. You can identify this situation if you find one chakra's color in more than two of your other chakras. In this case, a complete chakra reading/healing is called for, with specific emphasis on alignment and size matching, and special attention to the Gold Sun healing for chakras.

Now let's look at the possible meanings of other colors in your chakras. Be aware that bits or splashes of colors are not the same as an assist, which either shows up as a complete or partial wash of another chakra's color in the chakra you are reading.

COLORS

These are general ideas. Your own interpretations, of course, are the correct ones.

PINK: Healing humor, protection from abuse, indecision.

RED: First chakra, feet chakras, the physical body, power, anger, sexuality.

ORANGE: Second chakra, the emotions, the muscles, fury, sensuality, healing.

YELLOW: Third chakra, intellect, immunity and protection, impatience, fear.

GREEN: Fourth chakra, hand chakras, love, transformation, healing, frustration, loss.

BLUE: Fifth chakra, communication, spiritual knowledge, mourning, separation.

INDIGO: Sixth chakra, spiritual power, telepathy, victimization.

PURPLE/VIOLET: Seventh chakra, spiritual certainty, release, religious confusion.

BROWN: Feet chakras, earth energy, grounding ability, past-time issues.

BLACK: Finality, death, rebirth, delay.

WHITE: Spirit guide presence, purity, shock, erasure.

SILVER: Spirit-world information, ungrounded-ness, uncertainty.

GOLD: Hand chakras, eighth chakra, healing, neutrality, transformative illness.

In all cases, shade and energy are more important than color itself. If you have a fifth chakra that is all blue, don't think you're done reading. Is the blue pastel? If so, it can mean that your communication skills are pastel and filtered-out as well.

Is the violet in your seventh chakra very dark? Then your spirituality may be very dark and rigid. Does the emerald green energy in your fourth chakra sit there like stagnant water? Then the love you have is not as flowingly available as it could be. Does the orange energy in your second chakra career around like a pinball? Then your trapped and frantic emotions may need to be channelled.

If you sit with your chakras and let them speak to you, the colors will become only a portion of what you read. There are other things to see and feel. Colors are just a way to get into the whole chakra subject.

EDGES: The edges of each of your chakras should be complete and well delineated from the energy in and outside of them. I like to see chakra edges that are a darker or more vibrant shade than the color of the chakra itself. This helps the chakra remember who it is and where its energy is supposed to be. A pastel or indistinct edge creates a pastel and indistinct energy delineation, and chakra problems may follow.

The deviations seen in chakra boundaries are almost exactly like the ones seen in aura boundaries (see *Advanced Aura Reading and Definition* in *Rebuilding the Garden*), except that the information is more succinct.

A spiky aura boundary means that you are taking in too much energy and information, and that your aura can't cope, whereas a spiky second chakra boundary means that you are specifically taking in too much emotional or sexual energy. You can fix both.

A dent in the aura means that something outside of us is crowding and invalidating us, whereas a dent in the third chakra means that something is crowding and invalidating our thought process or our ability to create personal safety and power. That's much more specific, easy to look at, and easy to explore and heal.

If you need to know what your chakra edge problems mean, skip back to the section on aura boundary deviations in *Rebuilding the Garden*. Apply those definitions to your specific chakra's abilities and functions. Otherwise, re-form the circular edge of each of your chakras by visualizing them as whole, healthy, and vibrant in color and energy. You can use your hands to gently re-shape your chakras if your visualizations aren't clear enough yet.

If chakric edge problems are constant for you, you may not be quite centered and in your body yet. Please revisit all the early healing and meditation skills in *Rebuilding the Garden*, as well as this book's Gold Sun healing for chakras, and the chapter on cording.

ENERGY FLOW: Each of your chakras should be filled not only with color, but with a sense of flow or movement. Your chakra energy can swirl in circular patterns, bubble up and percolate, careen around and bounce off of its edges like a billiard ball, or flow in eddies and waves. In general, a constantly moving, medium-to-slow flow is best, but your chakras may have different ideas at different times on how fast, or in what pattern, their energy should flow.

The only real "must" about chakric flow is that it should be there. A completely still chakra, or a chakra made of glass or crystal, is a stuck chakra. If your chakra is perfectly colored, perfectly delineated, and perfectly shaped, but completely still, it is not healthy yet. Each chakra's energy must have movement and flow within it, or it will not be able to move, grow, and react appropriately to the changing energies in the world around it.

I see glass, crystal, and absolutely still chakras in early metaphysical students who become trapped in myths of spiritual perfection. Their chakras are perfect in every way, but framed and slip-covered to keep the dust out. I remind them that perfection, at least in its current definition, is static, and therefore not alive or vital. Wholeness, on the other hand, is lively, messy, and healthy.

Unmoving and unchangeable chakras cannot function (or help their owner to function) in the turbulent, living world. Chakras must be allowed to move with and react to the energies they encounter.

If you find no movement in one or more of your chakras, whether they are otherwise healthy or not, please place your fingers inside them and stir their energy around in a circular pattern. Remind yourself that a whole life has flow. A whole and healthy chakra system flows enough to roll with the punches.

During your Gold Sun healing for chakras (the next chapter), pay particular attention to running your golden energy through each of your chakras, stirring as you go. This will help them break out of the perfection trap and come into present time with you.

SIZE AND SHAPE: We've already gone over too-large and too-small chakras individually, but we haven't talked about shape yet.

All chakras are healthiest when they are circular, but chakras will transform themselves into bizarre shapes; sometimes because they are damaged, and sometimes because they are stepping into unknown territory. A quick way to determine if a strange shape is a healthy one is to look at the color and the edge of the chakra. If the color is correct for the chakra, and the edge is strong and unbroken, your chakra may just be opening to unusual information.

For instance, a new health regime that makes sense but goes against your schooling may cause your otherwise healthy third chakra to do a squashy contortion for a while until it digests the new information. Or, a previously abused and blasting heart chakra may distort itself in a number of ways as you bring it back to a healthy, balanced, circular shape. These distortions signal that you and your chakra have been off on a tangent for a long time, but that it is willing to ingest and accept your new, even contradictory information in order to get back into balance.

When your chakras are healthy but strangely shaped, you can ask them what's going on, but trust that they will bring themselves back to circular shape in time. If they are strangely colored or have compromised edges, though, they need to be re-formed and healed as soon as possible.

Misshapen and unhealthy chakras are signs of psychic injury, either from an unsupported, too-quick opening of the chakra's ability, or from abuse. Abuse includes consenting to cords, refusal to acknowledge the ability of the injured chakra, or that old devil, recreational drug use. All abuses can be stopped, and all chakra deviations healed.

If your chakras are unhealthy and misshapen, please go over all the early aura-boundary definition skills in Parts I and II of *Rebuilding the Garden*. Also, see the chapters on the Gold Sun healing for chakras and cording in this book. As you take back the energy of your injured chakras, make sure to use your hands in re-shaping and healing them. If your sick and neglected chakras know you believe in them, they will heal very quickly.

When you become proficient at reading your chakras, your Chakra Check and subsequent reading may be performed in a matter of minutes. As it was with all of our earlier skills from *Rebuilding the Garden*, our new chakra-care skills don't need to become a time-consuming burden.

When you have learned to channel your heart chakra energy into your hand chakras, and are consciously able to work with your own heart-love healing energy, this next chakra healing technique will make regular chakra maintenance swift and easy.

HEALING YOURSELF WITH YOUR HAND CHAKRAS

When your heart chakra energy flows down into your hands, you possess the perfect healing energy for your own body. Your heart energy, because it is neither a bodily energy nor a purely spiritual energy, is almost a neutral energy in your other chakras.

Heart chakra energy, in a healthy chakra system, understands the needs of the body and its chakras just as well as it understands the needs of the spirit and its chakras. This means that its healing assistance will not invalidate or confuse the body or the spirit, because fourth chakra energy doesn't take sides. Therefore, you can use your heart-connected hands to comfort a bruised shin, *and* a battered fifth chakra. Your healthy heart chakra can do it all.

Heart chakra energy is the best self-healing energy. There, I said it. Please notice that I didn't say that the heart chakra was the best chakra, the best energy, the best attitude, or the best healing for others. That would not be balanced or true. Heart chakra energy is the best energy to use in your own *self* healing—but only when your other chakras are aligned and working, your aura is whole, you are grounded and centered, you are aware that your heart energy is needed, and you are aware that you are using it.

In an unbalanced system, overflowing heart energy is a sign of general chakric distress. It's the sign of an unprotected third chakra, a corded fifth chakra, a sponging second chakra, an unaware sixth chakra, and so on.

In a balanced system, the regulated flow of heart chakra energy is a sign that self-healing is occurring on a regular basis, and that the spirit/body agreement is good. This is what I like to see.

Now that we realize a balanced and aligned chakra system is vital, let's learn to use our heart chakra energy in a way that will nurture balance, instead of abusing our heart and destroying it.

If you still haven't created a comfortable flow of energy from your heart chakra to your hand chakras, please skip back to the chapters on those chakras, and perform a few readings and healings on them, and on your system as a whole.

Please skip back to the early chapters in *Rebuilding the Garden* if this chakra information has confused and intimidated you. Remember that confusion means you're not centered, and probably not grounded either.

You're not a slow student. My grounding changes (and sometimes disappears) when I take in too much information. I also lose the room in my head, forget to destroy images, forget to burn my contracts, and refuse to channel my emotions sometimes. Hey, we're flawed humans, not androids. Lighten up and get centered. It won't take long to get yourself back on track.

When you have a comfortable level of control over your heart chakra energy, and you can open and close your hand chakras at will, you may notice that your right and left hand chakras run at different speeds or in different rhythms. This is natural, because the left and right sides of the body are not mirror images of one another. The left and right arms and legs are often different lengths. The left and right sides of the face are not identical, and in most people, one side of the brain, and its corresponding side of the body, is dominant.

By now, you know which of your hands is dominant. Mine is the right hand. If you stand at the top of a flight of stairs and step down with the leg that seems "right," you will find your dominant leg as well. Mine is my right leg. To round out the picture, you can also find your dominant eye. To do so, hold either arm straight out in front of you and raise your index finger.

With both eyes open, focus on a stationary object at least six feet in front of your raised index finger. Place your index finger square in the middle of your view of the far-off object. Close one eye. Is your index finger still lined up with the center of the object, or did your finger appear to move? Now, open that eye and close the other. What happened?

When you focus both eyes, one of them dominates, and your brain processes its information over the information of the subordinate eye. When you close your subordinate eye, the focal point remains virtually the same. When you close your dominant eye, your finger will appear to have moved away from the image you focused on.

Once again, my dominant eye is on the right side of my body, therefore, my right side is dominant, and energy will usually flow more freely from it than it will from my subordinate left side. If your dominance is on your left side, your energy will flow most easily from your left side. This means that your left hand chakra will be dominant, and that your right hand chakra will be subordinate. For me, it is the other way around.

If you have *mixed dominance*, with a dominant right leg, ambidextrous hands, and a dominant left eye (or whatever combination you find) your hand chakras will probably be able to trade dominant and subordinate chores. Keep this in mind as we begin to work.

During hand chakra healings, your dominant hand chakra will act as an energy transmitter, while your subordinate one acts as an energy receiver. When you sense a blockage in your body, your aura, or your chakra system, you will channel heart chakra energy into the blockage with your open, dominant hand chakra, to try and flush the blockage out. With your subordinate hand chakra, you will "catch" the channelled heart chakra energy until you sense that the blockage has cleared.

This is not a difficult process. The most important step is to know what your normal, healthy heart chakra energy feels like in each of your hands. When you know what "normal" feels like, you will recognize "abnormal" with ease. Let's try it.

Please get grounded and in your head, clean out your aura, and perform a Chakra Check. If you can ground by simply connecting your first chakra to your feet chakras, do that, and let go of your old first-chakra cord. When you are centered, please connect your emerald-green heart chakra energy to your hand chakras. Rub your hands together briskly until they are warm and tingly.

Bring both hands comfortably in front of you, and place your subordinate palm a few inches underneath and facing your dominant palm. Imagine the energy of your heart chakra intensifying along your dominant arm, and flowing freely from your dominant hand chakra down to the hand underneath it.

What can your subordinate hand chakra feel? Is it reacting to the flow with tingles, or a feeling of heaviness, or can it sense heat? Whatever you feel is right for you.

If nothing is happening, switch hands. Sometimes, your hand chakras work in their own universe, and don't care about your dominant side. Try again. Once again, this may take a while. Don't fret. Just keep working. You'll get the hang of this.

When you have a clear sense of your own heart chakra energy, in terms of its temperature, rate of flow, any sounds it makes, or anything else you perceive, you're ready to try your first experiment.

Choose a healthy area of your lower leg that feels absolutely fine right now, and use your hand chakras to channel your heart energy right through your leg. Place your open hands so that they face one another, with your healthy leg between them. Send energy through your leg with your dominant hand, and receive the energy you sent with your subordinate hand. Notice the changes your subordinate hand senses after your heart energy has passed through your leg. Did your heart energy slow down or speed up, change pitch, heat up or cool down, or push some energy out of your leg with it? If it didn't change at all, good. This energy flow shouldn't change in a healthy part of your body.

Did you sense a lot of changes, or lose the energy as it went from your dominant hand chakra and into your leg? If you did, your leg might have an energy blockage from an old injury. Channel more energy into your leg until your receiving hand chakra can feel the normal flow again. Often, your receiving hand will feel a big blob hit it, or it will be taken over with "pins and needles," and then the heart chakra energy will flow again and return to normal. This is what heart-connected hand chakra healing feels like.

If channeling energy through your healthy leg didn't affect your heart chakra energy flow at all, please move your hands to an injured part of your body and try the same healing. If your receiving hand chakra senses disturbances, intensify the flow from your sending hand chakra. When the flow of heart chakra energy feels normal to your receiving hand, the healing is over. Please shake off both of the hands like you do when shaking down a thermometer (this releases any trapped energy in the hand chakras), check your grounding, and go on to your Gold Sun healing.

When your body knows that its own heart chakra energy is available, it will wake up and suddenly remember all the pains you have ignored over the years. INCREASED PAIN AT THIS TIME IS NOT A SIGN OF FAILURE. Increased pain means increased opportunities for healing, and increased awareness within your body. Increased pain is a sign that you have graduated from our little beginning spiritual healing school. Bless your pain, honor it, and heal it. Your hands and heart have been waiting a long time to heal you. Let them. The pains will subside after you have dealt with them. They're only messages, after all.

After you learn to heal your body in this way, you can turn your attention to your chakras. During your regular chakra meditations, you can channel heart chakra energy through each of your chakras, and quickly heal them, too!

After you perform your Chakra Check and connect your heart chakra to your hand chakras, place your sending hand over your head, directly behind your seventh chakra. Place your receiving hand in front of your seventh chakra, with both palms facing one another, and channel heart chakra energy out of your sending hand chakra and through your seventh chakra. Let your receiving hand chakra catch the energy.

Is there a change from when your heart energy entered your seventh chakra to when it exited? If there is, your seventh chakra needs a healing. If the energy you sent in came out slower or colder, check to make sure that this chakra is the right color and size. This energetic slowness might signal an ignored aspect of your being that needs more attention right now. See if you can't get this chakra's energy moving a little better before you move down to the rest of your chakras.

If the energy you sent in came out faster or hotter, your chakra is working overtime. Check its boundaries to see if it is too open, and be on the lookout for its energy in your other chakras. It may be hyper-aware, and providing color assists for other troubled chakras in your system. See if you can't get it to calm down.

Did your receiving hand get hit with unusual energy, like a big blob, or a splash, or a bunch of sharp sensations? Then you may have cleared out a blockage. Your body may react in unusual ways. Your ears may pop, or you may belch or sneeze. Good. Your body is helping you by clearing out blockages of its own.

Does your receiving hand feel no energy at all? Then the chakra may be closed due to damage, or it could be taking a healthy chakra vacation. You know how to identify which is which.

If the chakra is closed due to damage, please place a healthy Chakra Check picture over it, and bless it as you go on to complete the rest of your chakra healing. When you are through, come back to the closed chakra. See if your work with the rest of the system has allowed it to open. If not, please read the chapter called *Special Topic: Cording.*

Continue on with your healing, and periodically run your hands over your arms. Check in on your heart-to-hand connection every now and then. Sometimes, trouble in a chakra can pull all the heart chakra energy back up into the chest. This is a normal reaction. Gently move the heart chakra energy back to your hand chakras, and keep working.

When you get to your first chakra, remember to re-connect your first chakra to your feet chakras. Even if the connection is already in place, it is thoughtful to include your leg and feet channels in any chakric healings you perform.

At the end of your healing, shake the excess energy off of your hand chakras again, and perform another Chakra Check before you go on to the Gold Sun healing in the next chapter. You're done!

Know that as you continue on with your chakra healings, your hands will become more sensitive. They will begin to know what pins and needles or certain temperatures or intensities mean. Don't be overwhelmed by all you don't know. Keep working, and you will become more proficient at deciphering the language of your energy body. If you need help, ask your little one (who is still safely sheltered inside the room in your head, right?) to take a look at your chakras. With a minimum of information, most children fall immediately into an understanding of the energy body. If you can get in touch with your younger self, you will also be in touch with your natural intuitive abilities.

As you move through your chakra system with this hands-on healing, your heart chakra energy will become intimately connected to each of your other chakras. This connection will help to raise your awareness, and your ability to balance and heal your body and your spirit. When your heart knows your whole being, its mediation skills will be strengthened. Your ability to live as a spirit in a body will be strengthened as well.

When your heart energy is used in this highest manner (on and for yourself and your specific issues), your ability to heal others will evolve in startling ways. You will become what I call an "invisible" healer. Your presence will bring awareness into those around you, who will suddenly need less—not more—healing energy directly from you. The people in your sphere will begin to grow up and take responsibility for their own pain.

Your heart chakra will suddenly understand, from within your well-modulated system, that some people cannot be healed, because they cannot take responsibility for themselves. Instead of trying to heal such people as you once did, you will bless them and move on. When you move on, these needy people will realize (on some level) that the game has been called. Then, their true healing will begin. When you are centered and aware, you will be able to heal some people by refusing to heal them! What a concept.

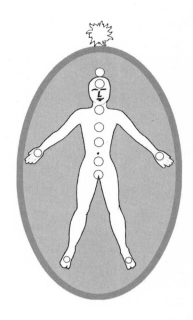

FURTHER INTO THE GARDEN

THE GOLD SUN HEALING
FOR CHAKRAS

This is a quick addition to your regular Gold Sun healing, and a very simple way to bring your chakras into alignment. When they are aligned, your chakras can maintain a healthy, flowing communication with one another. It is a very healing thing for your seven central chakras to be in conscious contact with your overseeing eighth chakra. When you can create a flowing communication in your chakric system, from the chakra at the top of your aura to the chakras in the soles of your feet, you will achieve balance.

If you can imagine a golden channel starting at your eighth chakra and flowing straight through your body to the center of the earth, you will understand your place as the mediator between earth and sky. You will no longer live in the world of either/or.

Once your chakras are lined up, you will often see them giving color assists to one another in times of stress. This is a hundred times better than having one surrender and close down while the others open too much in response.

After any meditation and healing session, Chakra Check, or chakra reading, please perform this special chakra alignment.

To align your chakras with Gold Sun energy, get grounded and centered. Call up your Gold Sun, channel it through your aura, and breathe it into your body in the usual way (see the chapter called *The Gold Sun Healing* in *Rebuilding the Garden*).

Now, create a solid ribbon (at least four inches wide) of gold energy from your sun chakra. See it coming down through your seventh chakra, entering your head and going through your sixth chakra, travelling through your skull to your throat chakra, and on down though your chest to your heart chakra. Allow some of the golden energy in your heart to travel down your arm channels and into your hand chakras. Stay in your head and watch the ribbon infuse each chakra with gold energy as it passes downward and on to the next chakra.

If you need to, you can use your hands to grasp the ribbon—to pull it down and guide it through each of your chakras.

Feel the golden ribbon moving down through your chest and into your third chakra at the solar plexus, through your second chakra, through your first chakra, and then see it continuing all the way down your grounding cord to the center of the planet. Allow some of the gold to travel down your leg channels and into your feet chakras as well.

When the ribbon reaches the center of the planet, allow gravity to tug on the ribbon and straighten it. There should be an absolutely straight path from your sun, down through all of your central chakras, and on down through your grounding cord to the center of the planet.

This straight-up-and-down alignment will help your chakras pass energy and information to one another—it will help to keep them all balanced and running at essentially the same size and speed.

Let this gold ribbon bring healing, present-time energy into each of your chakras for at least a minute, or longer if it feels right. Fill all of your chakras with flowing golden energy, and bring them up-to-date with your present-time healing information and abilities

When you are done, thank your Gold Sun and let it disappear. Close off the top of your head, close off the top of your aura, and let the gold energy drain out of you if it wants to. Bend over and touch the ground, and let your head hang down. Let your hands and feet come into contact with the earth after this spiritual healing. You may feel excess energy draining out of you, but if your body, aura, and chakras want to keep all the gold, you won't feel any draining at all. Stand back up, and you're done.

This Gold Sun healing can now be added to the one you learned in *Rebuilding the Garden*. This new healing should be used at the end of any sit-down meditation and healing session. It does not matter if you do a full chakra reading in each of your healing sessions; this chakra healing ribbon is always good for you. It is a healing in itself.

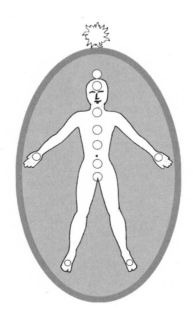

FURTHER INTO THE GARDEN

SPECIAL TOPIC: CORDING

Chakra cords are related to the relationship contracts we studied and destroyed in Part II of *Rebuilding the Garden*. Though this is an advanced topic, you now have an advanced set of skills that will allow you to look into the topic of cording in greater detail.

Cords of energy that flow from one person's chakra to another's are seen in all forms of contractual relationships. Cords can be created to gain clarity in a confusing situation where words don't work. They can also communicate love or concern, and they can be used to exert control.

Removing controlling cords from chakras is easy, because their presence usually brings forth a separation-supporting anger, or the original fear that probably allowed the cord-partner access to that chakra. Both emotions carry enough energy with them to make any separation work succinct and final.

When cords are placed or accepted out of misguided love or concern, however, they will be more difficult to remove. This type of cord comes from contracts entered into with much more willingness on our part than those we agreed to out of an unconscious, improperly channelled fear. Many people think concern-and-communication cords are okay to keep, because they are "nice" cords. I don't agree.

When we have cords, our chakras are being drained of energy, sometimes to the extent that they are essentially unavailable to us. It makes no difference at all if the chakra is being drained by a controlling molester, or by a confused friend or lover—the chakra is being drained. If we want to live whole and centered lives, a constant energy drain is a bad idea.

We need to have access to our own chakras, and cords interfere with that access. Cords can keep our chakras open in situations where they should be protected. Cords can also close our chakras down at times when they could be giving an assist to another chakra, or opening to allow a new stage of consciousness to manifest.

If you remember, it was hard at first to destroy people's images in our gift symbols. It's not supposed to be friendly to have privacy in our minds or our auras; however, we've seen that this privacy is irreplaceably vital to our well-being. Our "friendliness" actually trapped us and other people in old, inflexible roles.

It was also hard to burn relationship contracts, even our molest contracts, because we were taught that contractual obligations were more important than our needs, our health, our sanity, or even our survival.

Now we know that unworkable relationships and contracts imprison us in the past, and that we can easily live without them. Without the burden of contractual obligations, we absolutely thrive on relating from the present moment, with our immediate intuition and reactions. We live from our own truth, regardless of what others might expect from us, or how we behaved in the past.

Moving away from the bad psychic habit of cording is the same process. At first, it may feel as if you are betraying your cord partners when you stop playing the cord game. They will try to rope you back in with amazing tactics, they will play off your guilt, and they will pout. Most people do pout when they realize that they have to live their own lives and stay out of other people's spiritual territory.

I mean, it's much easier to cord into someone else's sixth chakra to figure out what they know than it is to come out and ask them. Early students try this on me, and it gives me a headache.

It's also easier to put a cap on someone else's seventh chakra (so they can't get to their own spiritual information) than it is to allow freedom of spiritual expression. Many religious leaders and gurus do this as a matter of course, but that doesn't make it right or exalted.

Cording is a form of communication for people who fear honesty, or who can't believe in themselves. It is an indirect, less-than-forthright way for people to connect when they cannot or will not trust in their human or spiritual relating skills.

Those of us who accept cords exacerbate our cord partner's poor self-image. We may think we're being loving and noble by allowing cord connections. We're not. We're only allowing a bad communication habit to perpetuate itself. We're only allowing people to remain frightened and helpless by buying into their old, tired stories.

When we try to throw cords into other people, we're saying that we can't get information for ourselves. We're saying we can't feel connected to people unless we've got tentacles lodged inside their chakras. When our cords are accepted, we have a contractual relationship right there, one that supports our idea that we are incompetent at speaking our truth, or unable to utilize our spiritual communication and separation skills.

When we accept cords, we agree that our cord partners are helpless, hapless, and incomplete without us. That's garbage all by itself, but when you add the fact that cording damages the chakra system and inhibits its functioning, there's no good reason to cord into others, except in one special instance.

There is a natural cord that exists between the first chakras of mothers and children, and sometimes between fathers and children as well. Birth mothers are naturally corded into their children during gestation, and adoptive mothers usually cord into their children as soon as they begin the process of bonding and nurturing.

Fathers may also cord during the process of bonding, but this does not always happen, probably because fathers so often get pushed (or pull themselves) out of the parenting process.

This natural cord runs between the parent's first chakra and the child's first chakra. It should stay in place until the child is thirteen years old. At that age (hopefully), the cord is severed. In many cultures, a separation ritual of some sort is performed at the age of thirteen, though usually only for boys.

The first chakra cord is in place so that the child, who is new at owning a body, can rely on the parent's physical information and grounding ability. If the parent is centered and grounded, his children will have a fairly easy time learning to live in their own bodies.

If the parent is not centered, and the information coming across in the first-chakra cord is not healthy, the whole process of childhood and child-rearing will be rather traumatic, especially as the child reaches adolescence.

If you've ever been around an adolescent, you know that her process is to separate from her parents. This can be handled with relative grace as the child takes on more autonomous tasks and living styles with a healthy parent, or it can be a numbingly wretched period of danger and disharmony in enmeshed and unhealthy homes.

When parents are able to clean out their own energy and stay grounded, the information that travels along their first chakra cord is something the child can use comfortably. When the parent is out of control, the child is fed confusing and even damaging information that gets in the way of his own growth. This confusion can create unconscious anger—even hatred—in the relationship. Both the child and the parent know on some level that the parent has failed. No amount of talking or therapy clears out the sense of betrayal on the part of the child, or the sense of shame on the part of the parent.

If your children are under the age of thirteen, you must be corded to them. The work you are doing now will help you create a cord with useful, uncluttered, and centered energy your children can use. When you dedicate yourself to yourself, miracles of healing and understanding are commonplace. When your energy transforms, the information travelling along your parent-child cord will transform as well.

Though your corded children may try to pull the stasis act at first, they will soon grow with you if you persevere. In growing with you, they will be more able to grow into themselves.

It is important to point out that children and parents may move their cords up into other chakras if the first chakra is closed, over-functioning, or filled with foreign energy (like molest contracts). This is not okay. The first chakra is the only chakra a child should ever cord into.

Children need information on how to live in a body. They do not need information on how to be exactly like their parents in emotions, personal protection, empathy, communication, and intuitive skills. They certainly don't need to have their parent's connection to God and the spiritual realm. All children need is thirteen years of gradually decreasing contact with their parents' first chakra energy. That's it.

If you find your children cording into any other chakra but your first, make sure your first chakra is clean. Then, firmly move your parenting cord down to your first chakra. Anchor the cord there, and run gold energy through the cord to the child to remind them that you are both now in present time, where bad cording habits are not acceptable. It may take a few times to break you and your kids of the habit of hopping around to your other chakras. Running your gold, present time energy along your correct first-chakra cord will help you both come into the present and accept new ways of communicating and functioning.

After you move your parenting cord down to your first chakra, check out the cording list later in this chapter to see what each of you might have been looking for in other chakras. It will help a great deal to picture both you and your children as healthy, complete, and spiritually intact. If your relationship is open enough, you might teach your children grounding and centering along with the Chakra Check. Talk to them about the work you are doing. In my experience, kids consider this work pretty natural, and they generally learn and incorporate it with a swiftness and ease that could make you feel a bit slow!

If your children are older than thirteen, you may still be corded in to them. This cord needs to be detached, grounded out, and let go of. If it isn't released, your teenage or adult children will be stuck in your life lessons and survival issues. If you are an adult still cording to your parents, you need to detach and let go of your cord as well. Instructions on how to remove cords follow my explanation of cording in each chakra.

SPECIAL TOPIC: CORDING IN INCESTUOUS FAMILIES

When incest exists in a family system, the cording between parent and child can be dangerous. The first-chakra programming in incestuous families contains a blueprint for abuse, enmeshment, punishment, disease, and insanity. How, then, can a member of an incestuous family break free and heal?

Incestuous families tend to raise martyrs who become physically or mentally ill, perpetrators who sexually or physically abuse others, or runaway healers who abuse themselves. Other unwell families encourage these roles, certainly, but incestuous families seem to have only these three choices. The parent-to-child cord is so unhealthy, and the programming is so very damaging, that children of incestuous families seem to have only two real choices: to hurt themselves, or to hurt others.

In such families, the first thirteen years of life can be seen only as a sacrifice. Children born into incestuous families sacrifice their childhoods, and often their health and sanity as well. And to what end? Probably as spirits, they saw the pain inside the family, and thought they could come in and heal it somehow.

Spirits think that way, you know. Because they have no bodies to make them think realistically, they are extremely foolhardy. You've got to love those wacky, heroic spirits. But, when you realize that you *are* one of those spirits, and that it was your decision as a spirit to come here and lead your family out of pain, there is only confusion. You got here, you were a helpless baby, your family was a group of dangerous, tragic nuts who had lost all touch with spirituality, and you ended up getting hurt with no way out.

Still, you most likely see the continuing tragedy of your family as your personal failing. Your mission in life was to come in and heal your sick family, but instead, you only seem to have provided them with another victim. Your martyrdom did not snap them out of their pain or their insanity. Now, you are hurt, and devastated by the belief that you have failed in your life's mission. You have a life, a sexuality, and a chakra system filled with crazy material, and after all the destruction, there is no relief—no happy ending—and no healing. How can you proceed?

You proceed by knowing that nothing can ever change your basic spiritual self. Nothing. When you arrived in your family, you came trailing energies and interests, realities and deep meanings, love and hope, and your specific way of looking at life. No one can ever take the deep and vital "you-ness" away from you. You are still the exquisite, foolhardy, brave spirit who wanted only the best for everyone in the world. You are still the spirit who was willing to sacrifice everything so that others could be healed.

Remember the chapter in *Rebuilding the Garden* called *Anger and Forgiveness*? I will remind you that forgiving your family before you have been sufficiently angry with them is a self-abusing act. Your family failed in their basic human duty to provide you with a safe home in an often unsafe world. Your family failed in their duty to love you more than they loved their various illnesses. Your family failed to see in you the spark of God's love, and to honor your very existence by caring for you. Your family failed you, and you have every right—even the responsibility—to be angry, furious, enraged, and sickened by their many, many failures. If you forgive them before you have charged them—really charged them—with a crime, your forgiveness will have no meaning whatsoever.

Premature forgiveness is a very dangerous thing. I have seen—time and time again—incest survivors who forgive their *mothers*, but then hate all women and distrust all authority figures. I have seen countless incest survivors forgive their *fathers*, then marry (or become) powerless, ineffectual men whom they ridicule and victimize in inhumane ways, because that's just how men *are*.

If your forgiveness pulls the blame off your abuser, but sprinkles it liberally over your world view, your forgiveness is a sham. If you can see the utter monstrousness of your male abuser, but are comfortable with your own masculine energy, and men in general, you are much further along in your process. If you can point at the disease running rampant through your family, but still envision a happy marriage and a disease-free family for yourself and other people, then you have triumphed, even if you haven't forgiven anyone yet.

The work here is to stop the martyrdom, once and for all. Premature forgiveness cements martyrdom, and leads away from the actual wounding of childhood assault. Premature forgiveness removes realistic footing and leads to an out-of-control, assaultive life experience.

People who forgive too early, who turn the other cheek (and then the other one, and then the other one), often slam into abusive people in the present, because they aren't looking where they're going. Premature forgiveness requires a psychic and emotional blindness that is dangerous. If you've chosen to be blind, your work will take a lot longer. Your path will be infinitely more painful than the path of someone who is willing to be honestly enraged at his incestuous family.

Without the strong, protective energy of anger, which is completely healthy and appropriate in an incest survivor, life is untenable. Without anger—properly channelled and consciously applied anger—self-abuse is certain. Without anger's barriers, an incest survivor will be unshielded and ripe for further abuse. Such a person will also be a danger to others if he doesn't know how to channel his emotions or uncouple from people in healthy ways. The dreadful lack of proper boundary respect within his sick family will translate itself into a poor or even dangerous lack of boundaries in his adult life.

Molest of any kind, by anyone, defies explanation; but molest within the family defies all the laws of God and man. The biblical injunction to honor the mother and the father, to respect the family without question, cannot be attached to a situation where the family acts in an unholy, unrighteous, and senselessly destructive way. An incestuous family that cannibalizes itself and flaunts all laws cannot run to the bible for protection from the real and righteous angers of its damaged offspring.

When I look at the pain in the eyes and heart of incest survivors, I see the beauty. I see them, still alive when so many others with their story committed suicide, or are committing suicide now with drugs and other abuses.

Incest survivors, I see you. Can you see yourself? Can you see the courage it took for you to get this far? Can you see that by not allowing your family's terrible legacy to kill you, you have ended the abuse in your lifetime? Whether your family members are still sick and crazy or not, you have ended the abuse in your lifetime, and that is all anyone can ever ask of you, God included.

I didn't want to bring God into this book in an obvious way, because so many people were molested by clergy members. These people *spit* at the mention of God, but your case is vital and special. Please forgive me for turning this non-denominational book into a religious tract, but in your case, and in the case of your injured child-selves, the mention of God is imperative.

In my childhood, my deeply religious neighbors were some of the most hurtful and evil people I have ever known. It was with very great trepidation that I approached God at all, but I kept trying to find Him all my life, in one place or another. I needed answers, and I needed them from the top! In my thirties, I decided to cut out the churchy middlemen, and ask God personally my questions about life on this often dreadful planet. I went out in my back yard and yelled at the sky. What I finally heard from Him surprised me. Instead of giving me biblical-sounding excuses for why I had to go through all the pain I experienced, he just sat with me and commiserated ... deeply, and with an ocean of feeling and understanding.

For me—startlingly, since I'd had a lifelong distrust of Christianity—the God who showed up was Jesus. For you, Buddha, Allah, Mother Mary, Kuan Yin, Horus, or Isis may be more comforting. But I tell you incest survivors—spiritual warriors one and all—no one knows more about the pain of giving His life to heal others than Jesus. And no one feels the pain of watching the cruelties of this world more than He does. He is the perfect person to talk to about what it means to be in pain, and what it means to fail in your mission to heal. The beautiful thing is that after you talk with Him, you won't have to go on with that painful life mission anymore. You've done your time, and you get a vacation for the rest of your life ... if you want it.

Even through all the pain, there has been something you loved to do—art, music, mathematics, fixing things—something. It is in that loved thing that your real healing energy resides, not just for people who are lucky enough to come into contact with you, but for yourself, for the planet, and for God as well. Your happiness will make God happy. Now, you get to take all your energy out of your sick, tired family system. You get to heal yourself, and head toward the thing that makes you most happy. Your martyrdom is over.

Here's the mantra for getting out of the trap of your family drama: *You are too important to God and to the world to spend any more time in anyone's unworkable drama.* If people around you are committed to being ill—if they are committed to a drama that will never change or end, this will now be your signal to leave. This wasn't your signal before, I know, but it is now.

Watch the people in your life and your family and ask yourself, "Do they want to be well, and if so, what are they doing about it? Do they keep doing unhealthy things time and time again—with no learning curve whatsoever? Is their drama more important to them than their freedom?" If it is, you don't have to be in their audience anymore. You don't have to be a part of that family anymore.

If, like me, you feel a need to have a first chakra connection to a better parental figure, to make up for the dreadful connection you got in your family, you can create a long rope out of your first chakra energy, and throw it up into the sky. Yell, "Hey, God! Catch!" Your God will help you, and will feed your first chakra strong, healing foundational energy. You can actually start over. It's never too late to have a happy first chakra.

WHAT YOUR CORDS MAY MEAN

As you move through your chakras, you will find cords. It's normal in this society where spiritual communication is ignored. For many people, cording is the only way they get fed, as it were, on a spiritual level. Now that you know this, you can show your cord-partners different ways to communicate as spirits—different ways to be fed.

You can now model grounding, being in the body, image-destroying, contract-burning, aura definition, and cord removal, too. Firmly removing cords will not only help each of you break a bad habit, but will move both of you forward in awareness, because the old game will be over. That boost in awareness is a real healing, and a real gift. Cording is neither.

If you want to know who is cording with you, light up the cord and see where it originates. Stay in your head. If you don't get a clear picture, grab the cord and pull on it a little. Someone will say, "Hey!" That's your cord-partner. If you can't figure out who your cord-partner is, let the cord go anyway.

It's not important to know every single detail about who, what, where, and why a cord is in you. It's just important to be aware of the cord and to remove it. Here are some ideas on why cords are in your chakras in the first place:

CORDS TO THE FIRST CHAKRA: Cords here are seeking basic information on survival and functioning. Your cord-partners may be grounding through you, or you may be trying to ground through them. These cords are only acceptable if they are running between parents and children under the age of thirteen. Otherwise, they can interfere with each partner's ability to ground, to survive on a basic bodily level, and to manage the bodily functions.

Some symptoms of first chakra cording are: grounding problems; unusually slow healing from illness or injury; unexplained cramping pains in the muscles and organs of the lower groin; and physical inability to relax during sex.

Molester Alert: molesters like to cord to the first chakra so they can control the bodies and physical sexuality of their victims. You can remove these cords very easily if you can get to anger or fear and channel those strong emotions into the severing process.

CORDS TO THE SECOND CHAKRA: Cords here are asking for emotional and sexual attachments or information. These cords also seek the total empathy we call *sponging*.

Some symptoms of cording in the second chakra are: diseases of the sexual organs; lower back or general muscular pain; uncontrolled sponge healing; or an inability to express the emotions, separate from the emotions of others, or function as an emotionally sexual person.

Molester Alert: molesters like to cord into the second chakra to control the emotions and gender sexuality of their victims. Helpful emotions to use in this cord-removal process are sadness and depression, because their watery energy helps wash the cord away. Fiery anger works well, too.

CORDS TO THE THIRD CHAKRA: Cords here seek control or information about power and immunity. Children will often cord parents here during conflict, so that they can gain control of the situation. Parents, you should move these cords down to your first chakra immediately. Be aware of keeping your solar plexus areas faced away from your child during discipline sessions until the habit is broken. Negativity-eating gift images (see *Rebuilding the Garden*) are very helpful tools in situations of third chakra cording.

Some symptoms of third chakra cording are: a lowered immunity to viral and bacterial infections; an inability to separate from other people or dangerous situations; mid-back or kidney pain; stomach pain and indigestion; or ulcers and hiatus hernias.

Molester Alert: molesters will cord into the third chakra when they seek total control of the thoughts and the psychic immune system of their victims. Often, molesting or controlling cords to the third chakra will bring forth panic attacks. If you can channel the intense energy of panic into the cord removal process, you will move on quickly.

CORDS TO THE FOURTH CHAKRA: Cords here seek love and empathy, and an understanding of how to connect the spirit and the body. Along with the whole fairy tale about the solitary greatness of the heart chakra, cords here are seen by some as a good thing. Once again, I remind you that the chakra system works best when in balance. Balance is lost when cords are present.

Focusing on one or two chakras (usually the seventh and the fourth) is a peculiar quirk of current New Age teachings, and it's one that causes a whole pile of problems. If you've got cords in your fourth chakra, they don't confer a special spiritual brilliance to you. They're just cords like any other.

Some symptoms of heart chakra cording are: pain around the upper back and sternum; angina pains and circulation problems; a spirit/body split you have to keep healing over and over again; a lack of time, love, and empathy for yourself; and an inability to bring healing love relationships into your life.

Molester Alert: molesters will cord to the fourth chakra if they seek forgiveness in order to continue their molesting habits without shame. If your molest memories are wrapped in bizarre professions of your molester's love and concern, you probably won't ever get angry at him or her. Drop the cord now and kick some psychic butt (see the chapter in *Rebuilding the Garden* called *Anger and Forgiveness*).

CORDS TO THE FIFTH CHAKRA: Cords here seek communication, either from or to you. These cords want control over what is heard or said. These cords want to hear everything first. They also want to get in the way of change and commitment.

Some symptoms of fifth chakra cording are: throat and neck pain; post-nasal drip; tinnitus (ringing in the ears) or hearing loss; an inability to understand others or speak up when you should; hearing voices; speech or hearing-connected learning disabilities; and an inability to commit to anything.

Molester Alert: molesters will cord into your fifth chakra if they want to keep an eye on your communications about them, and your commitment to healing. If they can keep you confused and full of brain noise, you won't have the quiet you need to tell your story, heal yourself, and go onward. Get into your head and drop this cord, no matter what the voices say.

CORDS TO THE SIXTH CHAKRA: Cords here want to know what you know without having to ask. Students will often throw sixth chakra cords to teachers, as will people who feel that they are in a one-down position. Cords here are also a way to deaden or control another's clairvoyance.

Some symptoms of sixth chakra cording are: behind-the-eye headaches; migraines; strange visions; eye or vision problems; reading disabilities; and dizziness or spaciness.

Molester Alert: molesters will cord into your sixth chakra if they want to make sure your memories and visions of them are hazy. They may psychically smack you if your clairvoyance begins to lead you back to them. Trust your intuitions and visions of the molest you experienced, drop the cord, and blow the molester away.

CORDS TO THE SEVENTH CHAKRA: Cords here seek to understand or control the connection to spiritual information. Many religious leaders or gurus will place cords or caps in the seventh chakras of their followers in order to keep out all conflicting information and to speed-load their own belief system into the follower. Sometimes, parents will cord into their children's seventh chakras in order to teach life or religious lessons.

Some symptoms of seventh chakra cording are: top-of-the-head headaches; a sense of detachment from the world or the world of spirit; an inability to contact spirit guides; and brain dysfunctions such as epilepsy or learning disabilities.

Molester Alert: molesters will cord into your seventh chakra to keep your spiritual healing energy away from you. Also, molesting clergy will cord here to keep religious fear and guilt active enough to bury the molest memories. Ask for help from your God in removing this cord, or channel one of the more certain emotions, like rage, terror, or suicide into your cord-removal process.

CORDS TO THE EIGHTH CHAKRA: The eighth chakra is safe from cording, but it will often appear to have cords flowing away from it. These cords are your Gold Sun's way of telling you your energy is someplace else. You can call the cords back to center each time you perform your Gold Sun healing. Since this chakra is the one chakra that *should* vacuum energy back into itself, cords here are normal and healthy. Just keep an eye on the number and thickness of these cords. Call your energy back and feed it to yourself and your entire chakra system as often as you can. Your Gold Sun healing is your best energy-retrieval tool.

CORDS TO THE HAND CHAKRAS: Cords to the hand chakras are there to understand or control one's contribution to the world. Some are placed by teachers of the arts or the healing arts so they can watch over how their student's energy is flowing during work. Some cords are in the hands to get a bit of heart chakra energy in a sneaky, roundabout way.

Some symptoms of hand chakra cording are: hand and wrist stiffness or discomfort; clumsiness with and constant injuries to the hands; an inability to feel energy flowing out of you; or an inability to make art, to heal, or to express yourself with your hands.

Molester Alert: molesters who cord to your hand chakras are usually family members who want control of the expressions you make in life. Unrelated molesters rarely care about what you do in your adult life, but incest perpetrators almost always do.

To remove these cords, use your hands to grasp and throw the cords down and away from you, and use your hands as much as possible in any separation, image-destroying or contract-burning. In essence, make your hands a tool of your strength and freedom, instead of a tool of the molester.

CORDS TO THE FEET CHAKRAS: Cords to the feet chakras are there to understand or control the connection to the earth. Sometimes, spirits new to this physical plane will cord to your feet to get an idea of what it feels like to have a body. I always tell them that having their own body is the best way to find out. Some people will cord into the feet to get a sense of grounding in secret, because foot chakra cording is not as noticeable as first chakra cording.

Some symptoms of foot chakra cording are: foot and ankle stiffness; clumsiness and foot injuries (constant toe-stubbing and tripping is a good indication of generally unhealthy feet chakras); difficulties with grounding; a sense of floating above the ground or the physical world; and an unwillingness to exercise (which might bring the cord up further into the body).

Molester Alert: molesters will cord into your feet chakras to pull the rug out from under you, as it were. By ungrounding you, they ensure that you will not have the ability to heal yourself and move on. Kick these cords away and spend some time in a Tai Chi or Aikido class if you can. Both of these disciplines rely on an awareness of the feet, and on the ability to ground.

A SPECIAL REMINDER: Of course, any of the symptoms of cording can be caused by completely unrelated, everyday health issues. I don't want you to run around like a loony, blaming your cord-partners for your kidney problems or epilepsy. I also don't want you to consider yourself a victim of their psychic bad manners. I'm going to write these next paragraphs in caps so you won't miss them.

WHEN YOU HAVE A CORD, YOU HAVE AGREED TO IT ON SOME LEVEL. NO ONE CAN CORD INTO YOU WITHOUT YOUR AGREEMENT. YOUR WORK IS TO BECOME AWARE OF YOUR ENERGY, TO TAKE RESPONSIBILITY FOR YOUR SIDE OF THE AGREEMENT, AND THEN TO HEAL YOUR PARTICIPATION IN THE AGREEMENT.

IF SOMEONE HAS PUT THEMSELVES IN A ONE-DOWN RELATIONSHIP TO YOU, AND ALLOWED YOU TO CORD INTO THEM, YOU HAVE AGREED THAT THEY ARE HELPLESS. YOU MUST BREAK THAT AGREEMENT. IF YOU ARE THE ONE-DOWN, CORDED-INTO PARTY, YOU HAVE AGREED TO SEE YOURSELF AS WEAK. YOU MUST BREAK THAT AGREEMENT.

CORDS ARE SIMPLY LEARNING TOOLS ON YOUR PATH TO WHOLENESS, AND SIGNPOSTS OF WHERE YOU ARE RIGHT NOW. YOU CAN CHANGE WHERE YOU ARE RIGHT NOW, AND MOVE ON. THANK YOUR CORD-PARTNERS. DO NOT HATE THEM FOR AGREEING WITH YOUR OWN VIEWPOINT. BREAK YOUR AGREEMENTS, BURN YOUR CONTRACTS, AND GET YOUR OWN ACT TOGETHER. MOVE ON WITH LOVE AND HUMOR, NO MATTER IF YOUR CORD PARTNER IS A FRIEND, AN ENEMY, OR A MOLESTER.

MOLEST CORDS AND CONTRACTS WERE CERTAINLY FORCED ON YOU DURING YOUR ASSAULT, BUT THEY CAN BE DESTROYED NOW THAT YOU ARE CENTERED AND SPIRITUALLY AWARE. REMEMBER THAT MOLEST CORDS AND CONTRACTS HAVE ONLY THE POWER YOU GIVE OVER TO THEM. YOU CAN TAKE THE POWER BACK FROM THE CORD AND USE IT TO EXAMINE AND BURN THE CONTRACT. YOU CAN USE THE POWER TO DESTROY THE CORD, AND TO HEAL THE CHAKRA AND ANYTHING ELSE THAT HAS BEEN INJURED BY THE CORDING. IT'S YOUR BODY, YOUR CHAKRA, YOUR ENERGY, YOUR HEALING ABILITY, AND YOUR DECISION.

REMOVING CORDS

To remove cords, please sit in your usual meditative state. Create both body and aura grounding vacuums to suck out old, unwanted energy. After a few minutes of vacuuming, you will follow with an aligning Gold Sun healing for chakras (including the hands and feet).

As you move gold energy into each chakra, ask to see its cords, if any. Ask to see who your cord-partners are. Some cords, especially long-standing ones, may not have a clearly defined partner. Your energy body may be so accustomed to the cord that it will forget where it came from.

Whether the cord partner is clear or not, each cord needs to be examined in contractual terms. It is often helpful to put the cord (and the attitudes you have toward it) into a contract and burn it as you allow the cord to detach and ground out of you. Your corded chakra may show you the discomforts and deviations the cord has caused. Your chakra will often brighten itself or speed up its flow to help you remove the cord. In many cases, the only work that needs to be done in letting go of a cord is to be aware of it.

When the light of your conscious, self-dedicated Gold Sun chakra hits cords, its present-time healing energy often disintegrates them without any further work on your part. Old cords aren't welcome in the present—they usually know that and scamper off. As the cords fall away, you can then envision a slippery, constantly moving film on the face of each of your chakras. This film will make your chakras too slick for any new cords to grab onto.

If you have children under thirteen, you must maintain your first chakra cord to them. When you get to your first chakra and remove any other cords, make sure to strengthen your parenting cord. Send Gold Sun energy along this cord to clean and strengthen it. After your cord removal process, check in on all your energy tools, plus the room in your head. Ask your aura if it would like a stronger Sentry system for a while. It might.

Sometimes, your un-channelled shame, fear, or anger will make it hard to get cords out of your chakras. These cords may need to be grabbed physically and dropped down your aura grounding cord. The skill of emotional channelling from *Rebuilding the Garden* is vital in this process. Often, when I am channelling my emotions, I will find chakra cords from controlling people (like my molester) who want me to remain unaware of—and unable to use—my emotions. In these cases, I make a tool (like a sword or a flame-thrower) from my emotional energy, and detach the cords with that tool.

For instance, my molester and I created a cord that made my anger very intense. I did rages or suicidal binges for years, neither of which helped me to grow or to understand myself. When I channelled my anger and found that it was bound up in a molest contract, I saw my molester cording my first through fourth chakras. I created a fiery red broadsword out of the anger and used it to cut away all his cords. I've also made rackety cord buzz saws out of frustration, ominous black cord guillotines out of suicidal urges, and cord-engulfing tidal waves out of despair. Channelled emotions are so useful!

After your emotional cord-removal, perform another Gold Sun healing for your chakras. Redefine your aura boundary and your Sentry system, and get into the room in your head. Don't be surprised or dismayed if you have to remove the same old cords more than once. Cording is a bad relating habit created and fostered over the span of your lifetime. The breaking of habits usually takes conscious application and reminders. Like any habit, though, this one can be broken.

Remember to use a complete, thorny, grounded Sentry blanket instead of a single Sentry in your first few un-corded days. You may need the extra protection for a while. Make sure that your Sentry blanket goes over the top of your head as well as under your feet, completely covering your entire aura. This will keep you separate from your cord partners if they try to re-establish their connections in roundabout ways.

It is also advisable to dedicate a feisty, free-roaming negativity-eating gift symbol to each of your once-corded chakras, so that you can have a constant Sentry system inside your aura. Because cording is often an unconscious action, it can help to have a part of your consciousness watching over your cording habit for a while.

After any cord removal, it is advisable to do another complete Gold Sun healing. This healing will pull your body, your chakras, and all of your energy tools into present time. Your Gold Sun healing, along with a re-dedication to your centering abilities, will alert your energy system to the fact that you no longer wish to link in unhealthy ways. Remember also to create a slippery, moving film over the face of each of your chakras, so that they are not easy to latch onto anymore. The Bach Flower remedies Crab Apple, Walnut, and Star of Bethlehem might also be very helpful at this time.

Though every energy tool is related and dependent on every other energy tool, the health of the chakras is vital in a well-modulated energy body. When the chakras are communicated with, aligned, healed, and honored, they will begin to offer wisdom and support in sometimes startling ways. In periods of quiet, your healthy chakras may actually speak to you, or tell you stories of the life you dream of. They will also be able to tell you how to get to that life.

When the chakras are balanced and working, you may find that your need for the external support of "experts" lessens. Over a period of time, you will begin to be able to do for yourself what you once had authorities do for you.

You may not need health gurus or doctors to tell you how to eat and when to exercise. You may be able to have less therapy, or less contact with career-and-life counselors. You may rely less on books, including this one, to tell you how to live. You may even find other people's psychic predictions unnecessary and uninteresting as your chakras begin to provide most of the information you need for your life and your lessons.

When the chakras are up and working in a grounded and centered body, all facets of life become connected and meaningful.

Trouble brings beauty, emotions bring healing messages and support, pain brings growth and deeply meaningful lessons, and happiness is no longer a mysterious, far-removed concept. When the spiritual body is connected to the physical, emotional, and intellectual bodies, all knowledge is available. All it takes is the willingness to live in and listen to the body, and to care for the mind, the emotions, and the spirit. When this balance is attained, life becomes balanced.

THE TROUBLESHOOTING
GUIDE

THE TROUBLESHOOTING GUIDE

It's me again, reminding you that more information is available. I've included this troubleshooting guide for you to leaf through if you have questions. I also remind you to go back to *Rebuilding the Garden* for the foundational skills of grounding, getting into your head, defining your aura, and separating from old energy patterns.

Of course, I can be reached, if your journey is carrying you away from beginning spiritual awareness and into more involved issues. If you can't find your answers here or in *Rebuilding the Garden*, please write to me at the address below. We can work together to create more clarity for you. Thank you.

Karla McLaren
c/o Laughing Tree Press
Post Office Box 1155
Columbia, California 95310-1155

THE TROUBLESHOOTING GUIDE

AURA: An area around any living organism that can be called "personal territory," often seen as a halo or aureole of colored energy emanating from the body. For general information on auric awareness and healing, please see *Rebuilding the Garden*.

AURA PROBLEMS: Chronic and serious aura damage or insufficiency is usually caused by damage from the environment, such as abusive and unhealthy living or working situations. If the aura is aware enough to break down in response to exterior stressors, it is on its way to a new life, which it will seek out by alerting its owner to what does and doesn't feel right.
Special topic: the aura can also break down in response to damage and deviations in the chakras. If your aura has broken down over the area of a specific chakra, this book will help you to heal and balance that chakra, and the chakra system as a whole. This will strengthen your aura.

BACK PAIN: In many cases, long-standing chakra cording or chakra damage will affect the physical body. Throughout the descriptions of each chakra and the cording process are examples of the kinds of physical pain most commonly associated with chakric disruptions. In the case of back, neck, or head pain at the site of the seven central chakras, a cord is often present. For help in removing such cords, please read up on the chakra that corresponds to your pain site, and then read the chapter called *Special Topic: Cording.*

BURNING CONTRACTS: When people enter into relationships, they often set up a series of postures, behaviors, actions, and reactions that can help the relationship to completely take over their lives. When such relationships and relating styles can be imagined as actual contracts, they can be brought into the light and into conscious awareness. Burning such contracts releases the energy that keeps people trapped in old behavior patterns. Burning contracts is especially good for removing reactions and behaviors learned during molest incidents. Please see the *Rebuilding the Garden* for specific contract-burning techniques.

Special topic: contracts can also take an energetic form, and appear as energy cords in your chakras. If your contract burning is not sufficient to release you from an entrapping relationship, please see the chapter called *Special Topic: Cording.*

CHAKRAS: Chakras are a series of energy centers in and outside of the physical body. Each represents a different aspect of the entire being, and each can be read, cleansed, healed of injuries, and brought into present-day awareness.

CHAKRA ALIGNMENT: The seven major body-linked chakras, which stack up in a line from the genitals to the top of the head, work best when they are in vertical alignment with one another. Aligning the chakras is a simple part of the special Gold Sun Healing for Chakras that is outlined the chapter of the same name.

CHAKRA COLORS: The seven major bodily chakras have specific colors that run up the vibrational spectrum, from red in the first chakra to violet in the seventh. These colors, as opposed to the often subjective colors in the aura, have specific purpose, meaning, and interpretation. Please see the chapter called *The Chakra Reading* for more information.

CHAKRA PROBLEMS: Problems in the chakras generally appear as shape and color deviations—these can be seen or felt in chakra readings and healings. Chronic chakra problems can signal health imbalances, drug damage, a long-standing acceptance of energy-diminishing chakra cords (see *Cords,* below, and the chapter called *Special Topic: Cording*), or a refusal to work with the leading energy of the damaged chakra.

CHAKRA READING: This is a healing technique for listening to the information of each of the chakras. Please see the chapters called *The Chakra Check* and *The Chakra Reading.*

CHANNELLING THE EMOTIONS: Though ignored, demeaned, and devalued, emotions are actually valuable messages from deep within the wisdom of the soul. When an inescapable emotional state is reached, channelling the emotion through the body, the aura, the chakras, and the grounding cord can bring absolute clarity and healing. Please see chapter of the same name in Part II of *Rebuilding the Garden*.

CLAIRAUDIENCE: The ability to hear psychic vibrations through the fifth, or throat chakra. Often, clairaudience, or hearing voices, is misdiagnosed as a precursor of schizophrenia. Please see *Ears* and *Ringing in the Ears*, below, and the chapter on the fifth chakra.

CLAIRSENTIENCE: The ability to receive psychic vibrations emotionally or empathically through the second chakra. Clairsentience can be a hazardous healing method when used outside of the immediate family, even for advanced healers. Please see the chapter on the second chakra.

CLAIRVOYANCE: The ability to see psychic vibrations through the sixth chakra, or third eye. Please see *Visions*, below, and the chapter on the sixth chakra.

COLORS: Colors are often valuable tools in readings, healings, and other spiritual communications, but they are very subjective. Below is a general overview of what colors may mean; however, personal definitions are always more valuable than any list made up by a complete stranger.
PINK: Healing humor, protection from abuse, indecision.
RED: First chakra and feet chakras, the physical body, power, anger, sexuality.
ORANGE: Second chakra, the emotions, the muscles, fury, sensuality, healing.
YELLOW: Third chakra, intellect, immunity and protection, impatience, fear.
GREEN: Fourth chakra, hand chakras, love, transformation, healing, frustration, loss.
BLUE: Fifth chakra, communication, spiritual knowledge, mourning, separation.
INDIGO: Sixth chakra, spiritual power, telepathy, victimization.
PURPLE/VIOLET: Seventh chakra, spiritual certainty, release, religious confusion.
BROWN: Feet chakras, earth energy, grounding ability, past-time issues.

BLACK: Finality, death, rebirth, delay.
WHITE: Spirit guide presence, purity, shock, erasure.
SILVER: Spirit-world information, ungrounded-ness, uncertainty.
GOLD: The eighth chakra, healing, neutrality, transformative illness.

COMMUNICATION PROBLEMS: Good communication is a natural part of working relationships, but communication skills can break down when relationship contracts get in the way (see *Burning Contracts*, above). Often, relationship contracts are unconsciously created to ensure safety and familiarity for all participants, but when growth occurs, contracts are usually not re-written. Soon, the relationship deadens and suffers from adherence to old rules and bylaws that do not apply to present-time growth, issues, or needs. In burning contracts, we learn to bring out, examine, and release all relationship contracts. We learn to be awake, aware, and healthy in each of our relationships, no matter how they made us feel and behave in the past. For information on contracts and their energetic manifestations, or *cords*, see the chapter called **Special Topic: Cording.**

CONTRACTS: See *Burning Contracts*, above.

CORDS: Cords are bands or tentacles of energy that connect people, usually through their chakras. Cords are the energetic form relationship contracts often take. Cords can be used for communication, control, or damage. In any case, they siphon energy from the physical and spiritual body and should be detached. For information on special, necessary cords between children and parents, and on cord-removal techniques, please see the chapter called **Special Topic: Cording.**

CROWN CHAKRA: Another name for the seventh chakra, which is an energy center located just above the head. Please see the chapter on the seventh chakra.

DISORIENTATION: A disoriented, forgetful feeling is generally a sign of being out of the body. Grounding and working through the beginning meditative processes outlined in *Rebuilding the Garden* will help to heal body/spirit splits that can lead to disorientations, as will healing and aligning the chakras. If you are consistently disoriented, please pay specific attention to your first and sixth chakras. It might also be a good idea to check in on the sections on *Kundalini* and *Kundalini Healing*, below.

Special topic: if you are in your body and you are still disoriented, you may have the room in your head too far up, which would center it directly behind your clairvoyant, vision-receiving sixth chakra. Please destroy your room and create a new one. Anchor this room below your eyes so that its ceiling is no higher than your eyebrows. Moving your room away from your sixth chakra will move you out of the psychic data-processing center, as it were. This should help to center and ground you.

DIZZINESS: Dizziness can be a signal of all sorts of medical imbalances that should be looked into; however, dizziness can also stem from being ungrounded, out of the body, and out of the room in the center of the head. Please read through the early portions of *Rebuilding the Garden* again, and see *Disorientation*, above.

EARS: The ears are energetically connected to the fifth chakra, and can sometimes pick up audible psychic transmissions. These can take the form of ringing or tinnitus, chronic ear infections, a constant need to pop and clear the ears, or hearing voices. The psychic skill of clairaudience (hearing voices) is a difficult one to possess, and since it is one of the leading indications of schizophrenia, it is also a difficult one to share with health professionals.

Without competent help or useful information, many clairaudients begin to perceive the voices they hear as directive—as if the information from the voices is their own, or God's, and should be acted upon. If an untrained clairaudient hooks up with unbalanced people or beings, and believes the perceived information to be an aspect of her own personality, chaos usually ensues.

All clairaudients require psychic training, specifically in regard to separating from the psychic information being received. This book can be used by clairaudients to center and separate from disturbing or uncontrolled psychic receptions. Please pay special attention to chakras four, five, and six, *Ringing in the Ears* and *Insanity*, below, and the chapter called **Special Topic: Cording.**

EMOTIONS: Emotions carry messages from the emotional body to the physical, mental, and spiritual bodies. Each emotion has its own purpose, voice, and character, along with specific healing information that can easily be accessed. The trick is not to express emotions all over the exterior world, or lock them away and ignore them as they fester. The trick is to use the emotions as healing energies. Please see the chapter in *Rebuilding the Garden* called **Channelling the Emotions**.

GOLD SUN: The eighth chakra, and the symbol used to depict the unlimited amount of energy available to each person on the planet. The Gold Sun chakra is used to re-dedicate the energy after a healing, to bring the body and all the energy tools into conscious, present-time agreement, and to heal the body. Please see the chapter called *The Gold Sun Healing for Chakras*.

GOLD SUN HEALING: See *Gold Sun*, above, and *Rebuilding the Garden* for a beginner's description of the Gold Sun healing.

GOLD SUN HEALING FOR CHAKRAS: An advanced but simple healing technique at the end of the Gold Sun healing which cleanses and aligns the chakras. Please see the chapter of the same name.

GROUNDING: An energy technique that helps to center the spirit in the body by centering the body on the planet.

GROUNDING PROBLEMS: Difficulties in grounding are common to survivors of childhood sexual assault, mostly due to the damage in the first and second chakras. Techniques throughout this book aim to address that damage, specifically through the cord-removal process in the chapter called *Special Topic: Cording*.

GROUNDING RULES: Grounding is the first step in this spiritual growth process, and with growth comes responsibility. Please see the section on specific grounding rules in *Rebuilding the Garden's* **Advanced Grounding**.

GROUNDING VACUUM: Grounding cords used for centering can be turned into energy vacuums used for cleansing. Please see the sections on the grounding vacuum in Parts I and III of *Rebuilding the Garden*.

HEADACHES: Beyond all the physical reasons such as illness, hunger, electrolyte and chemical imbalances, and tumors, headaches can be a sign of being ungrounded and out of the body, out of the room in the head, or out of contact with the sixth and seventh chakras. See the chapters on the sixth and seventh chakras, as well as *Special Topic: Cording*.

HEARING PROBLEMS: See *Ears* and *Clairaudience*, above, and the chapter on the fifth chakra.

HEART CHAKRA: Also known as the fourth chakra, the heart chakra is the energy center of empathic healing, spirit/body communication, and love of the self and others. Please see the chapter on the fourth chakra.

INSANITY: Beyond the more mundane, chemical-imbalance induced model of psychiatric disorder is the possibility of spiritual imbalance. Virtually ignored in psychiatric treatment are the possibilities of clairaudience in schizophrenics, trance-mediumship and *kundalini* problems in aphasics and seizure-prone individuals, and second/third chakra breakdown in depressives. One thing is certain: drug modalities and institutionalization have never proved worthy of the inexplicably hallowed place they hold in treatment of the disordered.

In my own bout with teenage depression and borderline schizophrenia, I found a wheat allergy, a severe niacin deficiency, an over-receptive fifth chakra, and a complete lack of grounding to be causal factors. Once addressed, my symptoms subsided, and I was able to heal in months two mental illnesses that essentially destroy entire lives in the Western medical model.

Though psychiatric drugs may help patients to relieve symptoms and deal with their underlying imbalance, drug use is often seen as a curative rather than a supportive measure. Many drug therapy support groups exist to provide succinct disease identification and techniques for the alleviation of drug side effects, instead of uncovering the real issues that led to the psychiatric illness in the first place. This is a part of the legacy of Western medicine, which is to find perfectly beautiful and properly spelled names for diseases without ever looking at the breakdown in life force that causes them. Holistic mind-body-emotion awareness is making an inroad into modern medicine, but the spiritual aspects of disease are still ignored.

Don't misunderstand me. Naming an illness is important, and Western medicine triumphs in that regard. After a while, though, being the bi-polar depressive in ward two, or the myocardial infarction on the table is limiting to the spirit. Knowing the name of the disease and treating specific symptoms is only a first step in the journey, not the be-all and end-all of healing.

There are no easy or miraculous cures for psychiatric disorders, but nutritional imbalances and spiritual injuries should always be explored. In addition, teaching the distraught person to ground, center, meditate, and heal their chakras and their aura would be invaluable. I have never seen a mentally disturbed person without a seriously disordered energy body.

Whatever the causal factors are in terms of childhood memories or other trauma, the symptoms of mental-spiritual disturbances respond far better to nutritional and spiritual intervention than they ever will to drug therapies and institutionalization. Plus, once the symptoms have calmed down a bit, correct body care and competent spiritual grounding will help the person to more easily explore and heal whatever it was that caused them to leave the "normal" world in the first place. Drugs and institutionalization cannot offer this support.

My suggestion for mental disorders in regard to this work is to go through *Rebuilding the Garden* in its entirety, mentally replacing the term "childhood sexual assault" with whatever trauma seems to have caused the current imbalance. I also recommend spending extra time and energy in this book, especially in aligning the chakras, and removing energy-scattering cords (see **Special Topic: Cording**).

INSOMNIA: When a child can't or won't sleep, it is usually because he fears missing out on something. It is the same with adults. Sleeplessness that is not caused by health or environmental disturbances generally stems from a gnawing lack of completeness or closure in situations or relationships. The body can't relax and let go because the day isn't really finished. In instances of sleeplessness, it is always good to ask, "What is still undone?" as you ground and get centered. The issue will usually pop right up, and the techniques of image destruction and contract burning will help to release energy from the issue.

Sleeplessness can also be caused by misalignments and disagreements between your third chakra's protective ability, your fifth chakra's communicative ability, and your sixth chakra's clairvoyant sense. Two or three of these chakras may be warring or chattering away, and keeping you awake to mediate for them. Please heal and align them instead, and see *Sleeplessness*, below.

Special topic: If your insomnia is of long duration, and you are edgy, uncentered, and ungrounded after a spiritual experience, you may have blasting *kundalini* energy that needs to be put back into your first chakra. Please read the chapter on the first chakra, and *Kundalini Healing*, below.

KUNDALINI: This is the Sanskrit word for first chakra energy, which is fiery and sometimes blasts itself upward into the other chakras during meditation or situations of immediate threat. Many spiritual practices encourage and manipulate these *kundalini* blasts, but if students are not advanced and centered, there can be serious difficulties. Please see the chapters on the first chakra and the connected feet chakras, and the *Kundalini Healing*, below.

KUNDALINI HEALING: When the energy of the first chakra blasts upward, it does so to clean out the other chakras momentarily, or to lend power to the body in situations of immediate threat. *Kundalini* energy is the energy in the fight-or-flight reaction, and the energy that allows 110-pound mothers to lift cars, trucks, or heavy machinery off of their children. It's that powerful. It's also damaging if it is allowed to blast for too long.

In many cases, molest victims will create disturbances in their grounding and *kundalini* energy by leaving their bodies frequently, and by using anger and rage inappropriately. Both of these less-evolved protection techniques can pull up the grounding cord and blast the *kundalini* upward. This is often the only defense many people have against brutality, or people who come too close. In such cases, calming the *kundalini* will be useful, but the fundamental grounding and centering work in *Rebuilding the Garden* should be mastered as well.

Too much *kundalini* can blast out the entire chakra system, burn holes in the aura, and shoot a person right out of her body. If too much *kundalini* blasts for too long, the body will even become damaged. Symptoms include dizziness and lack of appetite, insomnia, photophobia, waking dreams and visions, burn-like rashes, and tics and twitches that resemble St. Vitus' Dance. For general *kundalini* information, please read the chapter on the first chakra.

For specific help in calming a blasting *kundalini*, please re-read the *Kundalini Healing* in the Troubleshooting Guide of *Rebuilding the Garden*.

LIGHTHEADEDNESS: See *Disorientation* and/or *Dizziness*, above.

NECK PAIN: Pain in the neck, head, and shoulders can be a sign of difficulties with, or cording of, the communicative fifth chakra, which is located in the throat. Please see the chapter on the fifth and sixth chakras (they are often out of alignment with each other), and the chapter called **Special Topic: Cording**.

PANIC ATTACKS: Sudden rushes of panic, especially in response to innocent stimuli, are often signs of a heavily corded third chakra. For molest survivors, the cord-partner is usually the molester.

In the healthy third chakra, fear will come forward at appropriate times, and will ask for an emotional channelling session, or a simple shielding from the attacking person or situation. In a damaged and corded third chakra, the fear escalates into terror and panic. Because such cords keep the chakra stuck in past-time issues and assaults, it will often bring forward its terrors in response to bizarre and unrelated stimuli. This can make panic attacks very hard to heal in a psychological framework, where much time may be spent in identifying the present-time triggering events.

Fear and distrust are signals sent out by a third chakra at risk. Terror and panic are signals sent out by a third chakra in tatters. For help in healing your panic attack tendency, please read the chapter on the second, third, and fourth chakras, as well as the chapter called **Special Topic: Cording**.

REPRODUCTIVE ILLNESS: Imbalances of the reproductive organs are strikingly common to survivors of childhood sexual assault. So are lower back pains, bowel and colon disruptions, and digestive tract difficulties (all of which are at the sites of the first, second, and third chakras). When looked at in terms of spiritual wounding, chakric damage, and the possibility of cording with the molester, the energies of the illnesses are no longer mysterious. Though competent medical intervention will help to relieve symptoms, the energy underlying the lower-body imbalances must be addressed. Please see the chapters on the chakras nearest your site of disease or imbalance, as well as the chapter called *Special Topic: Cording.*

RINGING IN THE EARS: Ringing (or tinnitus) can have physical origins such as an electrical imbalance or misplaced vertebra. Ringing can even be caused by metal dental fillings that receive radio or television transmissions. Ringing in the ears can also be a sign that spiritual communication is being received and translated by the fifth, or throat chakra. Please see *Ears,* above, and the chapter on the fifth chakra.

ROOM IN THE HEAD: A meditative sanctuary created right behind the eyes, specifically for people who have maintained a long-standing spirit/body split. Please see *Rebuilding the Garden* for a description of this sanctuary. If staying in your room in the head is difficult, please make sure yours is centered below your sixth chakra (see *Disorientation* and *Dizziness,* above). Also, see that your Sentry and aura boundary systems are strong enough to give you some spiritual privacy.

SCHIZOPHRENIA: This is an incurable psychiatric disorder in the Western medical model. It is often linked to the misunderstood fifth chakra psychic ability of *clairaudience,* or hearing voices. Uncontrolled clairaudience is easily curable through the psychic healing techniques taught throughout *Rebuilding the Garden*; especially grounding, creating a room in the head, and burning contracts. Awareness of the fifth chakra is also vital. Please see *Ears* and *Insanity,* above, the chapter on the fifth chakra, and the chapter called *Special Topic: Cording.*

SLEEPLESSNESS: After all the physical causes are examined and discarded, sleeplessness can be seen as an unwillingness to doze off while things are undone and issues are unresolved. Sleeplessness is a good thing if it can be seen as the sign of a heightened awareness that will not allow one to be unconscious any longer; however, a sleepless body needs help. Please see *Insomnia,* above, and the chapters on the fifth and sixth chakras.

Special topic: as we learned in *Rebuilding the Garden,* sleeplessness can also be a sign of repressed memories of bed-or-night-centered molestation. Please go back to the *Garden*, and re-read the chapters *Creating a Room of Your Own*, and *Channelling Your Emotions*.

SOLAR PLEXUS: Another name for the third chakra, which is the center of the physical and psychic immune systems. Please see the chapter on the third chakra.

SPACINESS: This is a sign of imbalance in grounding, or in the chakra system. Please see *Disorientation* and *Dizziness*, above.

STOMACH PAIN: Fleeting stomach distress is often a request for protection from the third chakra. In such instances, the hands can be placed over the third chakra (which is in the solar plexus) while the aura boundary and Sentry are attended to. Chronic stomach pain, however, can be a sign of long-standing damage to the third chakra, or cording from controlling people such as molesters. Please read the chapters on the second, third, and fourth chakras, as well as the chapter called *Special Topic: Cording.*

THIRD EYE: Also known as the sixth chakra, the third eye is the energy center of clairvoyance and discernment. Please see *Visions*, below, and the chapter on the sixth chakra.

THROAT CHAKRA: Also known as the fifth chakra, the throat is the energy center of communication and clairaudience, commitment, and the ability to change. Please see *Ears* and *Ringing in the Ears*, above, and the chapter on the fifth chakra.

VISIONS: Visions are signs of activity in the sixth chakra, or third eye. If the visions are reasonably connected to your life, enjoy them. If they are unconnected and confusing or disturbing, please work through the chapter on the sixth chakra. Learn to read, heal, protect, and align your entire chakra system.

Special topic: if you have created a room in your head, and the visions started soon after, you have probably placed your room too high. You are most likely are sitting behind your clairvoyant, vision-receiving sixth chakra instead of behind your eyes. Please destroy your room and create a new one with the ceiling no higher than your eyebrows.

SUGGESTED FURTHER READING

HEALTH SUPPORT

Caroline Myss. *Energy Anatomy*. Six-tape audio series: Sounds True, 1995. Boulder, CO (800) 333-9185.

Mechthild Scheffer. *Bach Flower Therapy: Theory and Practice*. Rochester, Vermont: Healing Arts Press, 1988.

GENDER-BALANCE SUPPORT

Robert Bly. *Iron John*. New York: Vintage Books, 1990.

Robert Johnson. *He: Understanding Masculine Psychology* and *She: Understanding Feminine Psychology*. New York: Harper Perennial, 1977 (both titles).

Michael Meade. *Men and the Water of Life*. San Francisco: Harper, 1993.

Clarissa Pinkola Estes. *Women Who Run With the Wolves*. New York: Ballantine, 1992.

SPIRITUAL GUIDANCE

R.L. Wing. *The I Ching Workbook*. New York: Doubleday, 1979.

Shakti Gawain. *The Path of Transformation*. Mill Valley, CA: Nataraj, 1993.

Gerald Jampolsky. *Love is Letting Go of Fear*. Millbrae, CA: Celestial Arts, 1979.

Caroline Myss. *Spiritual Madness*. Audiotape: Sounds True, 1996. Boulder, CO. (800) 333-9185.

Robert Johnson. *Owning Your Own Shadow*. San Francisco, CA: Harper, 1993.

ACKNOWLEDGEMENTS

I'd like to acknowledge all the readers of *Rebuilding the Garden*. You were the people I dreamed of, meditated about, and spoke to when I was writing that book—and it was your energy that made *this* book possible. Thank you.

I also want to thank Dave Bonnot at Columbine Design for picking up the pieces, Thomson-Shore for being the most excellent printers and binders, Lisa Roggow at New Leaf Distributors for believing in *The Garden*, and Debra Evans at Whole Life Expo for believing in me. Thanks again to Suzan Still for insightful editing. The split infinitives are mine.

Special thanks go to Tino, Kara Hubbard, Kimberly Haskell, Pennie Austin-Wilson, Jennifer Hubbard, Anita Mukai, Fred Stephens, Lisa Ellerby, Pride Wright, Kathe Waterbury, Paul Patterson and Sarah Stone for supporting me through the tempests of promotion, travel, renown, and response.

Neverending gratitude to the Golden Man who gives heart transplants in the middle of the darkest nights.

ABOUT THE AUTHOR

Karla McLaren began a course of intensive spiritual study at the age of ten. She has now been a spiritual seeker, teacher, and healer for twenty-six years. Karla also began a professional writing career at the age of eighteen, and has won awards for her poetry, comedy, journalism, and ad writing. She lives in the foothills of the Sierra Nevada with her remarkable husband and her ever-more gargantuan son. *Further Into the Garden* is her second in a series of five books on spiritual healing.

DID YOU BORROW THIS BOOK?

You can order your own copy, or a copy of this book's companion volume, REBUILDING THE GARDEN: *Healing the Spiritual Wounds of Childhood Sexual Assault*, directly from Laughing Tree Press.

For FURTHER INTO THE GARDEN:
> Please send $9.00 ($7.00 plus $2.00 postage) to the address below. California residents, please send $9.50 to allow for state sales tax.

For REBUILDING THE GARDEN:
> Please send $13.00 ($11.00 plus $2.00 postage) to the address below. California residents, please send $13.80 to allow for state sales tax.

Address your orders to:

Laughing Tree
Press

Laughing Tree Press
Post Office Box 1155
Columbia, California 95310-1155